CHINA'S INTERNATIONAL BANKING AND FINANCIAL SYSTEM

CHINA'S INTERNATIONAL BANKING AND FINANCIAL SYSTEM

Paul D. Reynolds

PRAEGER

PRAEGER SPECIAL STUDIES • PRAEGER SCIENTIFIC

Library of Congress Cataloging in Publication Data

Reynolds, Paul D.
China's international banking and financial system.

Bibliography: p.
Includes index.
1. Banks and banking—China. 2. Finance—China.
3. Banks and banking, Chinese. 4. Banks and banking, Foreign—China. I. Title.
HG3334.R49 332.1′5′0951 81-17927
ISBN 0-03-056971-0 AACR2

Published in 1982 by Praeger Publishers
CBS Educational and Professional Publishing
a Division of CBS Inc.
521 Fifth Avenue, New York, New York 10175, U.S.A.

23456789 145 987654321

Printed in the United States of America

To my family

PREFACE

In the following pages I have attempted to summarize the banking and financial systems, as well as the policies and changes during the period 1978 through mid-1981. Those years were filled with startling reversals of traditional practices. They were marked by intense interest from outside China and a remarkable openness from within. Both factors have made this book possible.

In my research I have tried to keep in mind the needs of bankers and corporate planners as well as academic economists and lawyers. The emphasis is on systems, institutions, and broad policy, rather than on a detailed financial analysis, for which I am not equipped. Those seeking such detailed analysis need look to the assessments made by research departments of the major international banks as periodically updated or attempt to see the World Bank's June 1981 four-volume study. I have provided extensive references to assist those doing more detailed research than the ordinary banking or business reader.

When research for this book started in February 1979, official details of China's economy, in particular its finances, were only vaguely known. Information was scarce—often second or third hand. Detailed estimates were frequently uncorroborated or in grave conflict with each other. The trickle of information had started to become an onrushing stream.

Having opened its books, China threatens to engulf its students in a sea of statistics.* The flood tide continues to rise as this work goes to print. That so much information is available does not in any way make China more easily understood. Many gaps and ambiguities remain.

---

*These national statistics can still be quite vague. See W. Klatt, "China's New Economic Policy: A Statistical Appraisal," China Quarterly, December 1980, pp. 719-20.

Several preliminary observations are in order. The sea of figures from China is really too much to believe without a critical and even skeptical eye. Some figures are in conflict with others from the same source. Some claim growth rates that are doubtful. Indeed, the Chinese themselves have recently exposed the problem of exaggeration by overeager party workers. The speed with which some figures are released—for example, exports—is too quick to be accurate. Yet, the statistics are not labeled as approximate or estimates. In some areas there persists a remarkable degree of concealment—bits and pieces of information but not overall totals. This occurs in areas like the mining of precious metals, foreign reserves, settling of exchange rates, and balance sheets for domestic banks. Because of this the science of "economic archaeology," practices during China's relative statistical silence between 1957 and 1977, is still alive and needed.

Financial figures (for example, loans and prices) are given as reported unless otherwise noted. Values also given in other currencies are presented at the then-current exchange rates. Readers should note that no uniform exchange rates are used except as noted in certain tables.

Spellings of Chinese names and places in English are generally in Pinyin rather than Wade-Giles, except where the latter is used in a direct quotation or contemporary news account. Hong Kong and Macao use a variety of English spellings of Chinese words. Names of companies, persons, and places therein are given in the spellings most commonly used locally. The only spelling likely to cause confusion is Guangzhou, formerly Canton. In the notes and bibliography the source's original spelling is consistently used.

Historical material has been kept to a minimum. However, extensive references have been provided to older, original, and secondary source materials, so that those wishing to do so may refer back in time. All significant points are in the text. The notes are, therefore, for reference or minor clarifying comments.

London
June 1981

ACKNOWLEDGMENTS

Any lawyer who writes a book primarily involving economic, financial, and banking material risks a great deal besides the publisher's reputation. Praeger was supportive from the inception of this work, authorizing me to begin work on the basis of a four-page outline; few authors could have had as patient a publisher as mine.

A long-term project such as this required substantial support from several institutions. I owe a great debt to Texas Tech University and its School of Law. The former president, Cecil Mackey, and former dean of the School of Law, Frank Elliott, committed their respective institutions to support a trip to the People's Republic of China, Hong Kong, and London, as well as continuous support services, for over two and a half years. Edwin Lichtenstein of North East London Polytechnic offered aid, as did the firm of Fulbright and Jaworski.

My entry into the world of banking was eased by the benefit of the work and learning of others. As is conventional, the people who sacrificed hours and days to help me request anonymity. I am deeply grateful to these men and women in various Chinese cities—Hong Kong; London; Washington, D.C.; Houston; and New York—who made this a more accurate and acceptable book. Those who can be publicly acknowledged for their comments or assistance in providing original materials include Luc De Wolf, International Monetary Fund; David Denny, U.S. Department of Commerce; Francis Cheo, Monetary Authority of Singapore; Pauline Loong, Far East Economic Review; and Dick Wilson, London. A special thanks goes to the following readers of various drafts: Lynn D. Feintech and Tim Williams of the Bank of America and Professor Gordon Bennett of the University of Texas-Austin. I learned a great deal from their insights; but they are not, of course, responsible for any errors that remain, which are mine alone.

I wish to thank the staffs of the following libraries: Texas Tech University Law Library (especially Grace Lee and Carolie Mullens) and Main Library; School of Oriental and African Studies, London; Institute for Advanced Legal Studies, University of London;

Houston Public Library; North East London Polytechnic; and especially, the Society for Anglo-Chinese Understanding, whose friendliness and intimacy will be fondly remembered for years.

Many people rendered exceptional assistance in preparing and retyping the manuscript. Carla Callahan was there at the beginning and cheerfully helped until Pat Adams took over in London, assisted later by Sandy McDonald, Diane Shepherd, Pauline Creighton, and Eloyse Ewell. Several people assisted in the research, but Selinda Sheridan, doctoral candidate at Cornell University, and Louis P. Gregory, J.D., Texas Tech, were exceptionally diligent.

Finally, I owe a debt to Anne and my son, Niall, who patiently bore without complaint lost weekends, holidays, and long hours of early morning work.

CONTENTS

LIST OF TABLES AND FIGURE

LIST OF ACRONYMS

ADB	Asian Development Bank
ASEAN	Association of Southeast Asian Nations
BOC	Bank of China
CCC	Capital Construction Commission
CIA	Central Intelligence Agency
CITIC	China International Trust and Investment Corporation
COFACE	Compagnie Française d'Assurance pour le Commerce Extérieur
DM	deutsche mark
ECGD	Export Credits Guarantee Department
Eximbank	Export-Import Bank of the United States
Ex-Im Bank	Export-Import Bank of Japan
FCIA	Foreign Credit Insurance Corporation
FIC	Foreign Investment Commission
FTC	Foreign Trade Corporation
GAEC	General Administration of Exchange Control
GNP	gross national product
ICBOC	International Commercial Bank of China
IDA	International Development Agency
IFO	International Financial Organization
IMF	International Monetary Fund
JVL	Joint-Venture Law
JVs	joint ventures
LIBOR	London interbank offered rate
MFN	most-favored-nation
MOF	Ministry of Finance
mmt	million metric tons

OCIC	Overseas Chinese Investment Company
OECF	Overseas Economic Cooperation Fund
PBOC	People's Bank of China
RMB	renminbi
ROC	Republic of China (Taiwan)
SEC	Securities and Exchange Commission
SDR	Special Drawing Right (international monetary unit)
UBAF	Union des Banques Arabes et Francaises
UCP	Uniform Customs and Practice for Documentary Credits of the International Chamber of Commerce
UNDP	United Nations Development Programme
UNDRO	United Nations Disaster Relief Organization

1

OVERVIEW OF THE ECONOMIC, MONETARY, AND BANKING SYSTEMS

ECONOMIC SYSTEM AND POLICY

China's economic and monetary policy is dominated by politics. Even with the present pragmatists in power, domestic and foreign financial decisions are dominated by politics rather than scientific management. The present government is often said to aim at depoliticizing economic life. Its actual record shows that strong political struggles are raging. After all, Chinese history is replete with examples of the ongoing struggle between those devoted to Confucian orderliness and acceptance of roles and those influenced by a Taoist leaning toward anarchy—something at the heart of the Cultural Revolution.[1] Being political, present policy and institutions are thus changeable and subject to sudden reversals. This is not necessarily wrong. It is, however, essential to an understanding of the current system and an appreciation of the role China's foreign bankers and financial decision makers play today—roles that will continue to evolve quickly. The continued evolution will not go unresisted. Each two steps forward may be followed by one step backward, before another two steps forward can be attempted.

How then does one sketch an overview of the economic system upon which China's foreign banking and financial system is based?

It appears that all one can do is to give the broad outline of the main themes in changing policy. In doing so the reader is advised to seek detailed discussion of the economic system in two forthcoming publications—Audrey Donnithorne's China's Economic System (revised edition) and the Joint Economic Committee's update study on the Chinese economy.[2]

THE FOUR MODERNIZATIONS

In 1978 China made a bold commitment to rush into modernization by the year 2000. The start was an ambitious Ten-Year Plan to recover ground lost during the previous tumultuous decades. Four areas were targeted: defense, science and technology, education, and industry. Some 120 major projects were scheduled to be under way by 1985, including several new ports, pipelines, oil fields, and a comprehensive series of iron and steel works.[3] The vision of a new China launched on the long road to modernization captured the imagination of the press and people around the world. It also brought forth a wave of unrealistic euphoria from businessmen in the West who expected vast new markets to open up and huge contracts to be quickly concluded. In its initial states it strongly resembled the oft-used mass campaign rather than a gradually and carefully worked out plan.

READJUSTMENTS

The realization in May 1979 of a large budget deficit in 1978, and that even larger ones were likely in 1979 and 1980, caused consternation in China's political decision-making bodies and among economic planners. The latter may well have foreseen and appreciated the potential long-term benefit from medium-term deficits. But many political leaders were shocked. What power plays went on has been the topic of continued speculation. A clear result, however, was the abandonment of the Ten-Year Plan and its replacement by a much less ambitious and interim Three-Year Plan. The interim plan was to be replaced by a revised and more realistic set of objectives for the subsequent five years.

The Communist party revealed in May 1979 that, despite earlier claims of agricultural growth and self-sufficiency, population growth was outstripping food production. New plans involved increased investment in agriculture. Earlier emphasis on heavy industry and capital-intensive production was causing another problem, namely aggravation of already serious unemployment, officially put at 20 million in early 1980. Each year 7 million school children graduate, and only 300,000 to 400,000 go on to higher education.

Within several more months it started to become obvious that the previous emphasis on heavy industry, combined with the autonomy of enterprises and provinces, had resulted in unforeseen and uncontrolled overordering of advanced plants and equipment from Japan and the West—so much so soon that there simply was not sufficient infrastructure or capacity to efficiently absorb the plants. Nor was there sufficient foreign exchange to pay the bills.

This was a critical point in economic decision making. As will be seen, China had by mid-1980 either arranged or been offered abundant foreign credits to pay for the equipment ordered or being delivered. The moment called for an economic decision to accept medium- to long-term debt and the problems of absorption and to invest in industry that might provide the capacity to fuel growth and pay off the loans. That decision was not made. It may have been wise economically, but the prevailing view is that the decision was made for political reasons. As is discussed in detail in Chapter 5, the doctrine of self-reliance is deeply ingrained, and it was felt that continuation on the existing plan was not acceptable. Foreign debt of the order then required was viewed as foreign dependency.

Apparently, it was only in 1980 that policy makers became fully aware of the disproportionate share of total capital investment being absorbed by heavy industry (55.5 percent, compared with 5.15 percent by light industry). At the same time, it was realized that light industry was earning a return so rapidly that initial costs were recouped within two years (versus 16.5 years for heavy industry), and that light industry was providing profits to finance 97 percent of China's investment in industrial capital construction.[4] Policy makers did the obvious and sacrificed some prestige heavy-investment projects to emphasize light industry instead.

Since early 1979 the specific plan of action set in 1978 has been first reconsidered, then readjusted, and finally, redefined altogether. This shift in priorities and pace is still continuing in mid-1981.

DECENTRALIZATION AND DEPOLITICIZATION

Traditionally a centrally planned economy, China is trying to decentralize implementation of broad national plans. Power and responsibility for economic management is being placed with economic organizations, not with party officers or administrative bodies. At the same time, much planning and significant management are being shifted downward from the national level to more local levels. The issue of decentralization of economic management has arisen often in China's modern history.[5] Each time a reaction against excessive decentralization has set in. This time the program appears to be giving provinces or groups of provinces more independence in implementing economic goals, that is, the freedom to use the enterprises and methods they feel most appropriate as long as overall general goals are met. Those goals now give great emphasis to "budgeting accruals" or profits. The difference is twofold—more emphasis on profits and enterprises are permitted to retain large portions of those profits to use as they see fit, whereas previously these had to be totally surrendered to the state. The central government also retains a general planning and coordinating role, especially in allocating resources, but even the latter has loosened up to allow local flexibility. "Self-management" is the new slogan.

Successful economic decentralization depends upon good local management willing to take on responsibility. Despite welcoming back former private businessmen, a real shortage of good managers exists and will persist for some time. Willingness in others is not present. Having been persecuted before in China's periodic political upheavals, they are victims of "lingering fear" and are slow to jump on the new bandwagon of profits and pragmatism. Finally, in a country the size of China new policies and training take a long time to trickle down, if they ever do.

The implementation of this policy has also been plagued by uncertainty and self-doubts. In 1978 enterprises were told to increase exports and were promised they could, in general, retain their foreign currency earnings to do with as they pleased. By late 1979, however, the State Council decided that new, stringent exchange controls were needed to curb spending and borrowing of foreign exchange; it set up an institution to coordinate and license how retained foreign exchange could be spent. This is only one example of the tentativeness with which the process is being approached. This may be necessary, but it is hardly conducive to long-range planning by industry or encouraging to wholehearted commitment by local management.

One way that oversight and indirect central control can be maintained is through a program of building up the domestic banking system (by, among other things, substituting loans for grants and making enterprises justify their loan proposals instead of seeking government grants) and the tax system. These programs are elaborate and have been written about elsewhere.[6]

PRIVATE ENTERPRISE

Several private enterprises are being encouraged—partly to absorb the unemployed and partly to satisfy consumer demand.[7] Restaurants, photographers, repair shops, and peddlers have blossomed. Free markets have grown where commune workers sell produce from their private farm plots.

PRICE REFORM

The reform of prices is an enormous problem.[8] At present, prices in many industries are still subsidized or fail to reflect the true costs of raw material or labor. As a results, profits for some industries have been highly inflated, while other sectors have long been kept in artificial poverty. Attempts to reform prices have thus far had some negative effects. Inflation was set off by a sudden increase in agricultural prices for several staples. Until December 1980 many industries were given freedom to set prices according to market forces, but this clearly contributed to inflation. Prices remain frozen, although some modest changes occurred on selected items in late 1981. Further price reform has been postponed until late 1982.

THE MONETARY SYSTEM AND POLICY

The monetary system in China today still bears a strong resemblance to that of the USSR in the 1940s. That country's system of political and economic organization provided the early models for China's leaders to use after the People's Republic was founded. It was, therefore, natural that the basic structure of China's monetary system closely followed that of the USSR.[9] The Chinese diverged from the Soviet model where they felt that the differences between Soviet and Chinese economic development made such adaptations necessary. The Soviets were not pleased with the initial variations on their model, and these divergencies caused the two nations to criticize each other's monetary and economic planning systems and thereby contributed to hostility between them. Recent, more radical changes by China away from the Soviet model can only lead to further Soviet charges that China is turning toward capitalism.

Monetary policy has consistently focused on three immediate goals: controlling inflation and its causes, promoting savings to maintain a high rate of investment, and keeping enterprise spending within planned allocations.[10] These themes are dealt with separately here but should be kept in mind collectively when considering the structure and roles of China's banks.

Currency

Chinese leaders understand the value of a stable and unified currency. They demonstrated this knowledge during the Revolution by using currency in economic warfare. As the Communists captured territory, they confiscated Nationalist government gold yuan notes. These were passed to Communist agents in cities still held by the Nationalist government; the notes were used to buy rice, cotton cloth, woolen goods, drugs, and other daily essentials. The agents paid three to four times the market prices, driving prices up further and thereby fanning the flames of inflation.[11]

During its early days the Communist party, through its agencies and controlled banks, issued many different currencies, so that by the mid-1940s 20 kinds of Chinese Communist currency were in circulation. The monetary history of this confused era is documented elsewhere.[12] The need for a unified currency became obvious. On November 22, 1948, the People's Bank of China (PBOC) and the new People's currency were established; the latter was said to be backed by food and cotton, not precious metals or foreign exchange.[13] The new replacement currency was exchanged for all existing currencies in circulation. Shortly after the successful Revolution, the Communists unified the new currency, calling it People's currency or renminbi (RMB).

At present the basic unit is yuan, represented by the symbol ¥.* It is the sole national legal tender. Yuan is issued in small denominations of note and coin. This makes the regulation of hoarding, exchange control, and counterfeiting somewhat easier. One reason for withdrawal of large denomination notes, in circulation before 1964, was fear that the USSR might smuggle large amounts of counterfeit currency into China, repeating the successful tactic used by the Chinese Communists themselves during the Revolution.

Cash and Credit Control

The first task that confronted China's new leaders after the Revolution was combating, and ultimately controlling, inflation.[14] From the very beginning, economic planners established systems of cash control and credit planning. Currency was the only liquid asset in the Communist economy that was not controlled and could, therefore, bid up prices or create excess demand. The central object of the banking system was to recapture the largest possible portion of currency put in circulation. Today the most closely watched part of the credit plan is the increase in currency circulation, which is planned in conjunction with the cash plan.

Cash Controls and the Cash Plan

The government declared a cash-control system built around the PBOC in April 1950. All government offices, state enterprises, and cooperatives had to deposit all their cash (currency) with the bank. In July a decree ordered these same organizations to turn all cash receipts into the PBOC on the same day they were received, and generally, no more than three days currency requirement was to be retained as petty cash. In January 1951 the system was completed by ordering all transactions between socialist enterprises be done via direct bank transfers and not cash. No mutual credit or deferred payments between such enterprises were permitted, and

---

*The subsidiary units are jiao (ten jiao = one yuan) and fen (ten fen = one jiao). The form of expression is RMB ¥1,000.55, or renminbi one thousand yuan, five jiao, five fen.

proceeds of state, semistate, and cooperative enterprises had to be deposited with the PBOC.

The annual cash plan of the People's Bank was the outline of its effort to maintain monetary balance under which cash originated with the bank and, after limited circulation, returned to the bank.[15] Today, the bulk of cash still enters the economy only through wage payments to households and sales of agricultural products on free markets. All transactions, except those involving consumer purchase of goods and services, are made through book transfers at the PBOC. Individuals may have savings accounts but are not permitted to have current checking accounts. Most transactions are noncash, with transfers or settlements representing 85 percent of the total PBOC transactions in 1959 and 95 percent in 1979.[16]

Most observers agree that the purchasing power of the currency has, until recently, remained quite stable—especially when compared with prices in the West. The system was designed, however, to cope with necessary adjustments when inevitable imbalances occurred between the supply of cash and the availability of state-fixed-price goods and services.

In theory any errors that put an excess of cash in circulation were easily correctable. Excess cash could be absorbed by increasing retail sales prices, public utility charges, service industry charges, or by making savings and bonds more attractive.[17] Today, these sources of cash receipts together account for about 85 percent of total currency inflows and are, therefore, still the main channel for withdrawal of currency from circulation. The first alternative of increasing prices turned inflation into its own cure. However, psychological and political consequences made authorities reluctant to use such measures in the past.

In general China has used rationing instead of price increases, but only as a temporary measure until equilibrium between supply and demand could be restored.[18] Rationing has, however, persisted to the present day. Taxes could also be raised to counter excess cash. Such increases were largely unacceptable for the same reasons as price increases. In practice, China has focused upon intensifying savings deposits and bond sales. Party cadres were used to exhort the population to save more or, when bonds were issued, to buy more. When the process of exhortation was carried to excess, the savings drive became a thinly disguised direct tax.

Credit Controls

Credit controls operated directly and indirectly. By law, state agencies, enterprises, and cooperatives were prohibited from extending credit to each other.[19] All cash was to be deposited with the banking system; it worked with the relevant government agencies to control and allocate credit. Government agencies obtained funds by direct state appropriation. Enterprises, cooperatives, and communes received direct grants and loans. Banks supposedly ensured the operation of controls by allowing cash withdrawals only for wage payments approved within plans and by requiring profits, taxes, and depreciation funds to be returned to the treasury each year. In theory, enterprises had to turn to the authorities for approval and funds to meet long-term capital requirements. Short-term loans by banks were permitted where credit had been preapproved, a repayment schedule agreed upon, and the loan secured by work in process or finished products.

Controls in Actual Practice

The system sounds excellent and would warm the heart of any modern monetarist. But for the system to work properly, several factors must come together. Planning, particularly of supply and demand, must be in balance. Cash controls and accounting standards must be adequate in and of themselves. Cash and credit controls must be complied with. Banks must operate controls according to plan and free of political pressure. However, the Chinese admit, and today freely cite, examples of imbalance. Many of the present leadership's reforms are premised on past imbalances from faulty planning: increased supply of consumer goods, higher wage levels, free markets to increase agricultural supplies, and the introduction of two-tier foreign exchange rates for RMB. Continual readjustment of the timing for achievement of the Four Modernizations has unquestionably been necessary and has been caused by continued failure within the planning system.

Bankers also openly talk of being pressured and bribed to ignore credit controls by managers desperate to increase production at all costs. Some Chinese bankers have stated that, "the leadership is usually interested in the problems of production, marketing, and trade, but seldom in problems of banking" and "if the bank worker disagrees with anybody, he is often accused of 'sabotaging production' and 'sabotaging the market.'"[20] Other accounts describe public denunciation, unlawful imprisonment, arrest, extortion, and family persecution. The slowness, and in some cases failure, to comply with controls has led Dwight Perkins to observe that "financial regulations were among the least obeyed of centrally issued legislation."[21]

The currency-control system as outlined was never fully implemented or enforced through a comprehensive plan for source and uses of funds.[22] There is also substantial evidence that accounting standards were not adequate. China now acknowledges that enforcement was very lax until 1960, and that controls broke down again during the Cultural Revolution. Through 1980, funds have flowed to certain economic sectors in a frenzied or haphazard manner. The most erratic extremes were during the Great Leap Forward and the Cultural Revolution, and while China has tried in recent years (especially in 1979 and 1980) to come to grips with this enormous task, official news accounts almost daily expose examples of the system simply breaking down. The Four Modernizations and Period of Adjustment are the battlegrounds on which the financial-planning war is being fought.

Savings

Other than gold, jewelry, or heirlooms, the only outlet for private savings are bonds and savings accounts at the PBOC or the Agricultural Bank and its rural cooperatives. Savings will have to provide a major portion of the capital required for modernization. Capital formation through savings has been one of the success stories in Chinese economic history since the Revolution. While savings rates declined slightly in 1977 and 1978, a campaign to encourage saving has been highly successful since 1979. The Chinese people have a high propensity to save despite their relatively low per capita income.

A domestic savings policy has important implications for foreign financing. One of the reasons China was forced to reschedule or cancel several major contracts in 1980 was not because of a shortage of foreign exchange (China had negotiated but not used large and cheap Japanese supplied credit); it was because of a domestic deficit. That deficit was largely attributed by the government to runaway capital-construction costs. Therefore, an increased and continually stable savings program is important to China's international financial position, because it contributes to China's ability to provide the local-cost portions of major projects

TABLE 1

Total Volume of Personal Savings, 1978-80

	1978	1979	1980
Savings (RMB millions)	24,000	28,000	39,900
Rural	n.a.	7,800	12,100
Urban	n.a.	20,200	27,800

n.a. = not available

Sources: Xinhua News Agency reports on January 31, 1981 and April 3, 1980; and *Economist*, May 9, 1981, p. 106.

utilizing foreign equipment. Savings and bond purchases are not obligatory by law or regulation. Deposits are transferable to heirs and are free of tax. Considering the growing economy, little inflation, and stable currency, such accounts have been perceived by the Chinese, including those overseas, as an attractive and secure investment. An average of 4 percent of employees' wages are deposited, the bulk into time deposits. Interest rates have increased several times in recent years to raise the total volume of savings and attract longer-term deposits.

Table 1 shows that 1980 savings by volume increased 42 percent over 1979, with urban savings increasing by 38 percent to RMB 27.8 billion (U.S.$17.37 billion). The total number of accounts increased in 1980 by 15 million to total 100 million.

A high rate of savings must be partially attributed to a scarcity of certain staples. With limited supplies of consumer goods, savings may have increased because there were few alternative uses for funds. In May 1979 the vice-premier, Li Xiannian, publicly stated that 10 percent of the population had too little to eat and that rice rations had fallen to 31 kilograms (from 41 a few years ago). It is also known that per capita cloth production, and thus probably supply, has declined dramatically.

Given the past astuteness of bankers in raising the rate of savings and the natural proclivity of the population to save, there is every reason to expect further success in this field despite the impact of recent inflation. The role of savings in the formation of investment capital has been minimized by at least one authority who states that while savings totals have steadily increased "their relative proportion of total revenue is still small."[23] Thus, the role of financial institutions in mobilizing investment capital has been minimal, especially when compared with a capitalist economy. That is less true today. If measured against revenues (for example, total 1980 savings of RMB 39.8 billion against total revenue of RMB 106 billion), savings are clearly a substantial proportion. If measured against the 1981 capital-construction budget of RMB 32 billion, savings are at quite adequate levels. Even the net increase in savings of RMB 11.8 billion in 1980 could finance a third of the capital construction in 1981.

Inflation

Ravaged by inflation during World War II and afterward, post-revolutionary China's most pressing problem was restoration of economic and monetary stability. During the Revolution, already severe inflation went totally out of control. The Nationalist government's control of the economy slipped away with its political control of mainland China. As the Communists swept through the countryside, the government's main source of revenue—the agricultural tax—was progressively lost. The Nationalists responded by keeping the printing presses running, a policy that threatened to undermine the military success of the Communist armies. From May 1946 to May 1949 wholesale prices in Shanghai, for example, rose seven and one-half million times.[24] The shocked reaction of the revolutionary government was to adopt a severe but highly orthodox program, which made great progress in reducing the rate of inflation by 1950-51. Monetary stability had been restored by 1952, having been accomplished in several stages.

Controlling inflation in any developing nation—indeed one must today say in any of the world's nations—is never an easy task. This makes China's rapid success all the more surprising, particularly so because the government has been able to achieve a high rate of growth without significant price increases. Past inflation has been modest and under control. It remains to be seen whether this is true of the current surge in inflation.

Current inflation was set off by badly needed changes in wage and price levels in the agricultural sector and the introduction of the bonus system in industry. The restructuring and shift to a general-market orientation caused substantial deficits in the 1979-81 budgets. Such deficits are not in themselves a bad thing for a developing nation, especially one with China's potential, yet it came as a great shock to the leadership. It goes against a long tradition, as well as conventional Maoist orthodoxy. It must have caused a great deal of turmoil within the government and pressured them to cut back. In any event China now acknowledges it has inflation (6 percent per annum during 1980), and moreover, has acknowledged that it has been circulating excess currency in 1979 and 1980. By the end of the first half of 1981 the PBOC was able to announce withdrawal of RMB 3.98 million from circulation—RMB 1.5 million more than was withdrawn during the first half of 1980.

To decide what to do, a national conference on prices was held in February 1980.[25] The need for the continued restructuring of prices must have been argued, and while the need for reform of prices was obvious, many planners must have also argued for greater caution in revaluing the economy. Price-control programs were authorized with the aim of stopping the chain reaction set off by agricultural price increases in 1979. Initial price controls introduced by local governments were generally ineffectual; by December 1980 Deng Xioping felt it necessary to impose a nationwide, six-month price freeze, thereby stalling his own efforts to revalue price levels through market forces. The freeze applied to both state industries and cooperatives. Having cleared up the symptoms, it remains to be seen how the government will treat the causes of current inflation.

FOREIGN MONETARY POLICY

Balance of Payments

China was a net earner of foreign exchange from 1958 to 1978, if invisibles are included. Foreign trade was, however, a very modest percentage of the total gross national product (GNP), generally under 2 percent. That percentage was 5.3 by 1979. Table 2

TABLE 2

Foreign Trade, 1976-80
(billions of U.S. dollars)

	1976	1977	1978	1979	1980
Total trade (fob/cif)	13.3	15.2	21.1	27.7	40.6
Exports (fob)	7.3	8.1	9.9	13.0	19.7
Imports (cif)	6.0	7.1	11.2	14.7	20.9
Trade balance	1.3	1.0	-1.3	-1.7	-1.2

cif = cost, insurance, and freight
fob = free on board

Sources: U.S., Internal Working Paper, February 1980; Report of Vice-Premier Yao Yilin to August 30, 1979, session of National People's Congress; State Statistical Bureau communiqué, released by Xinhua News Agency on April 30, 1980; U.S., Central Intelligence Agency, China: International Trade, Fourth Quarter 1980, Research paper (Washington, D.C.: CIA, May 1981), p. 30.

the rapid growth in trade; both imports and exports are striking. Imports grew faster than exports, and the rate of growth in exports slowed in 1980 and the first half of 1981. China's 1979 trade deficit was virtually offset by surpluses in the first half of 1980. However, the trade budget for the latter half of 1980 grossly underestimated existing and pending commitments. The year-end deficit was first announced as RMB 800 million, but this figure was later revised upward to RMB 1.9 billion (U.S.\$1.26 billion). Preliminary Central Intelligence Agency (CIA) estimates for 1981 place the trade deficit for the first quarter of 1981 alone at U.S.\$440 million.

The reaction to these trade deficits, which were public knowledge (itself as unusual change from past years), was particularly strong and similar to the reaction to the domestic deficits. Possibly there was overreaction. At first, wholesale cancellations and deferrals of many major contracts for plants and equipment were announced. This caused a great lapse in the goodwill that the post-Gang of Four government had enjoyed from foreign firms and banks, particularly those of Japan. The steps were reconsidered, and gradually several major contract works were renewed or rescheduled for completion six months to a year after the original dates. This is an ongoing process and remains in quite a state of flux. Among the fairly definite elements of the government's plans are the following: increased textile and consumer-goods exports; drastic cutbacks in the cash portion of China's foreign aid program (previously significant[26]); and tighter enforcement of foreign exchange controls to prevent large, unapproved orders for equipment by provinces and industries. Attempts to increase income from invisibles are discussed in Chapter 7, as is the restructuring of export/import policy.

Foreign trade is still conducted in accordance with an annual foreign trade plan drawn up by the Ministry of Foreign Trade in conjunction with the State Planning Commission. The ministry issues directives on the plan's preparation to all Foreign Trade Corporations (FTCs) and foreign trade bureaus in the provinces, regions, and municipalities, which in turn solicit views of interested parties. Lists of needed imports and goods available for export are prepared. From those lists local plans are prepared. The ministry and commission then balance and coordinate the competing plans. The annual national plan is to put to the State Council for its final approval.

Closely linked is the annual plan for foreign borrowing. All FTCs, municipally owned enterprises, government agencies, and cooperatives wishing to borrow abroad must prepare a plan showing the kinds of imports for which loans are intended. These proposals must show the applicant's foreign exchange earning potential and repayment ability. The State Planning Commission cooperates with the Foreign Investment Commission (FIC) in reviewing these proposals. For large-scale capital construction the Capital Construction Commission is involved.

These bodies weigh China's current National Development Plan priorities, the proposed projects' ability to rapidly repay the loan, and the overall debt-service ratio of the nation. Most borrowing is done through Bank of China (BOC) loans. Certain national enterprises and provincial entities are permitted to borrow directly abroad with or without a BOC guarantee. Direct borrowing by entities other than the BOC requires approval, in the first instance, by the General Administration of Exchange Control and the

FIC, and in the second place, by the State Council. These steps also apply, under the foreign exchange regulations described below, where the Chinese entity proposes to issue securities for foreign exexchange.

Reserves

Official reserve figures have not generally been available in recent years, but it is obvious that as China borrows on international capital markets—through government credits, loans from commercial banks and international agencies, and bond issues—accurate information on its reserve position will become more important and be demanded by prospective creditors. It was thought by some that upon entry into International Monetary Fund (IMF) membership this information would become available. If it has, it has not been made public on an official basis. This follows the example of another member, Romania.

In July 1978 Vice-Premier Li Xiannian informally revealed that gold and foreign exchange reserves totaled over U.S.$2 billion.[27] It was thought that one-half of that was in gold and, thus, was subject to the particularly large fluctuations in gold prices since 1979. By late 1978 most estimates ranged from U.S.$4 billion to U.S.$5 billion. In the 1950s the hard currency portion had been held in sterling, but in 1965 China moved into Swiss francs and precious metals.[28] Presently, a variety of currencies are being held; the largest portions are believed to be in U.S. dollars and yen.

The trade deficits of 1978 through 1980, about U.S.$3.5 billion, must have been met partly out of reserve as well as by foreign loans and invisible earnings. The resultant drain on reserves contributed to the decisions in December 1980 and February 1981 to cancel or postpone a large number of major-project contracts that had outstanding foreign-currency balances of between U.S.$700 million and U.S.$800 million. Therefore, it is uncertain how much credit should be given to Vice-Premier Yao Yilin's November 7, 1980, statement that reserves totaled more than U.S.$6 billion.[29] The Bank of International Settlements records showed only U.S.$1.3 billion net deposits with Western banks at that time, therefore gold holdings would have to be valued at nearly U.S.$5 billion if Yao Yilin's statement was correct. It must be said that no reliable estimate of reserves is presently available.

Invisible earnings are known to be substantial, having grown recently, and show great potential. Some of these—tourism, gold purchases, and remittance income—are considered separately in Chapter 7. Finally, gold production is also up and continues to make a large contribution toward the buildup of reserves.

International Settlements

Socialist Trading Partners

China's trade with other centrally planned economies is understandably highly structured, taking place via formal trade agreements.[30] Those agreements often establish trade clearing accounts between the central bank of the trading partner and the Bank of China (although formerly with the central bank, the People's Bank of China). The purpose is, of course, to settle payments, and from the Chinese viewpoint, to help control the balance of trade and preserve foreign currency. The pattern is similar to those used by Eastern European nations. The IMF listed China's bilateral payments agreements (clearing accounts) with 18 IMF members and 10 socialist states.

These accounts are normally opened with each other for one year, and all payments for the year are made through them. Sometimes several accounts are established—a main account for trade and several special-purpose accounts (for example, postal or shipping payments). These accounts are denominated in Swiss francs and settled and closed at year-end, though some agreements permit payments to be made for an additional month. Surpluses are transferred to next year's account to be paid and settled within one to three months. During the year, deficits may have occurred, and agreements with some nations (for example, the USSR and Poland) call for interest payments on the overdraft. Interest only becomes due when an agreed margin is exceeded or the overdraft has lasted beyond varying time limits.

The accounts have used a wide variety of currencies. In the 1950s and 1960s Soviet rubles were popular with pounds sterling gaining in popularity until devaluation forced a general switch to Swiss francs. Occasionally RMB or the currencies of both parties are used. Trade contracts under the agreements almost always require prices to be changed as the official rate of exchange of the designated currency fluctuates against gold. This has necessarily changed since gold was demonetized by IMF member nations in 1972, the effects of which neither world markets nor socialist countries could avoid.

Historically, the People's Republic has stated a preference for barter, since, by definition, trade on this basis is in balance. While some examples of this preferred means of settlement can be found, China's trade partners have not widely accepted the offer.

Capitalist Trading Partners

With some capitalist nations, particularly with developing nations, such as Burma, Syria, and Egypt, or Scandinavian nations, such as Finland, trade also takes place through structured trade agreements with settlement arrangements not all that different from those with centrally planned economies.[31] Settlement agreements with developing nations often use the opposite country's currency. This concession is not always disadvantageous for China.

Most major capitalist trading partners do not have settlement agreements, payments being made through mutual accounts between the BOC, on the one hand, and numerous private banks, on the other. Traders may also arrange payments through accounts maintained with overseas offices of the BOC and its subsidiaries. A variety of convertible and nonconvertible currencies have been used in recent years. Pounds sterling predominated until 1967 when the Swiss franc and Japanese yen were briefly tried. By opening RMB accounts with foreign correspondent banks in 1970 and denominating export contracts in RMB, China pushed its own currency as a medium of exchange. By 1971, 26 non-Communist countries, including most of Europe, were using RMB to some extent. This usage has, however, declined in recent years.

China's main trading partner, Japan, has used a series of settlement agreements concluded between the BOC and the Bank of Tokyo. These agreements changed slowly over the years as experience clearly demonstrated that a new approach was necessary. In the middle of 1975 a new currency exchange agreement with Japan was signed in Beijing,[32] which provided for the BOC and the Bank of Tokyo to accept yen-RMB transactions up to six months forward when backed by actual trade contracts.[33] The two banks also agreed to convert the existing Japanese trade surplus in RMB into U.S. dollars instead of into pounds sterling. Since then, Sino-Japanese trade has continued to grow rapidly, and Japan remains China's largest trade partner. Dollars were favored by China because in 1975 it perceived dollars to be a weak currency compared with yen and, thus, preferred to risk dollar depreciation during its deficit with Japan.

U.S. dollar settlements and payments were difficult because of the looming legal cloud of U.S. claims against China and the resultant Foreign Asset Control Regulations. Payments were, therefore, handled by foreign banks with U.S. branches (for example, Alegmene Bank Nederland and Banca Commerciale Italiana in New York or Canadian Imperial Bank of Commerce in Portland, Oregon).[34] Even after the foreign-assets settlement agreement was signed between the United States and China, and after full correspondent relations opened up between the BOC and U.S. banks, most payments were still cleared in this way. This was because individual U.S. banks had to reach their own frozen-asset agreements with the BOC after the government-to-government agreement. Most U.S. banks involved signed such agreements around December 1979 or January 1980. Only since 1980 have payments and settlements been handled directly by the major U.S. commercial banks, and in these China's settlements with non-Communist nations follow normal practice.

Exchange Rate Policy

The promotion of RMB as an international currency, particularly through its standard trade contracts and international settlements policy, was a goal for some time. This, of course, would have reduced the risk to China of foreign-currency devaluations, but these efforts have met with only limited success as few major contracts were denominated in RMB. Factors in this lack of success include China's overvaluation of the RMB exchange rate, refusal to provide a forward market beyond six months, and failure, until recently, to disclose reserve and balance-of-payments figures. Some of these problems will hopefully be overcome through compliance with the requirements accompanying membership in the IMF. China may, however, elect, as has Romania, to keep some or most financial details confidential between it and the IMF. The establishment of the General Administration of Exchange Control (GAEC) in 1979 may also lead to clearer foreign exchange policy. It is discussed below, but thus far it has not contributed to a successful and steady foreign exchange policy.

It is difficult to say in 1981 how or by whom the exchange rate is set, even if it is not difficult to find numerous conflicting sources on these points.[35] One or more of four agencies are said to be involved: the PBOC, the GAEC, the State Council, and the BOC. It is clear that exchange rates are set each day and that they are altered broadly in line with important world events and changes in the international monetary system. They are published by Xinhua News Agency, state radio, and at BOC branches. Precisely how China fixes its exchange rate is not known. Several studies have made educated guesses.[36] Officials have recently said in public and in private that a formula based on a basket of hard currencies is used and that the object in fixing the spot and forward rates is to keep RMB stable vis-à-vis a basket of currencies. The following factors are considered: the general monetary situation, the relationship between soft and hard currencies, the index of living standards, inflation, and world prices. The author's best understanding of the procedure for fixing the rate is that the State Council periodically approves a formula to be used in establishing the daily exchange rate. It acts upon the recommendation of staff of the General Administration of Exchange Control, who probably consult the BOC and the PBOC or, if not those banks, submit their views directly to the council. The BOC applies the formula each day. It has been said that this is done without daily consultation or approval of the PBOC and the GAEC. After the BOC president signs the order, it is taken to the State Council's office for its formal approval, and, strictly speaking, the rate is set each day by the State Council. This summary must be treated with caution, however, because both the GAEC and the PBOC have stated their roles in more direct and exclusive terms. The ambiguity here, even amid sources within the government and its agencies, is not uncommon. This is just one of many aspects of China's banking and financing system that is simply unclear. The IMB's first Annual Report on Exchange Arrangements and Exchange Restrictions, dated 1981 and which included China, rather vaguely states that the exchange rates are published by the GAEC without explaining how the rates are arrived at.

There have been some charges that the setting of the exchange rate is arbitrary and changes too frequently. Not until August 1974 was a split rate for purchases and sales of RMB established with a spread between the buying and selling rates of one-half of one percent. Its intention in making this change was unclear, but the simplest explanation is that a profit on the transactions was possible, and foreign exchange reserves could be increased. Another explanation might be in China's desire to reduce any incentive to buy and sell RMB deposits for speculative reasons within the narrow market permitted. Finally, it could represent a desire to make RMB appear more similar to other world currencies.

In the early 1970s China began to provide a limited forward market to traders in several European countries in their local currencies against RMB. No market was available in yen or dollars, a fact that caused great hardship to Japanese traders. This, combined with the frequency and apparent arbitrariness of rate changes, upset the Japanese. Apparently the size of Sino-Japanese trade seemed too great a potential exchange risk to China for some time. It was not until mid-1975 that a yen forward market was created.

At that time a forward marketing for U.S. dollars of six months became available, with rates starting at 0.6 percent for one month and rising to 3.0 percent for six-month advance purchases. In 1977 the rates ranged from 0.9 percent for one month to 4.0 percent for six months, and in 1979 from 1.2 percent to 3.0 percent. As of December 31, 1981, China offered a forward market in 15 currencies: Swiss francs, deutsche marks (DM), Japanese yen, U.S. dollars, pounds sterling, Dutch guilders, French francs, Hong Kong dollars, Austrian schillings, Belgian francs, Canadian dollars, Danish kroner, Italian lire, Norwegian kroner, and Swedish kroner.

As of January 1, 1981, spot exchange rates are published daily for 25 currencies: the 15 listed above and Australian dollars, Finnish markkaa, Ghanaian cedis, Guinean sylis, Iranian rials, Mali francs, Pakistani rupees, Sierra Leonean leones, Singapore dollars, and Tanzanian shillings. Forward rates may be offered for new currencies, including some of these 10, if trade in a particular currency increases sufficiently to justify the market. However, little use seems to be made of these limited forward markets because of the high premiums charged and the fact that China now denominates most contracts in hard currencies. These markets have not been limited to interbank trading, because companies in large transactions, including U.S. companies, have been allowed to conclude forward contracts directly with the BOC.

Devaluation

Some commentators, particularly the Japanese, felt that the RMB exchange rate may be set too high, thereby overvaluing its China currency. Support for this view was found in the growing problem of a currency black market, which was countered by the introduction of a special scrip for foreigners to act as a foreign-currency certificate. It has been estimated that the real value of the RMB is only one-third to one-fourth of the official rate. Some tourists have been offered nine times the official rate.

The State Council announced a two-tier exchange rate in December 1980—a measure that caused enormous controversy.[37] At that time the official rate of exchange with the dollar was approximately U.S.$1 = RMB 1.50. The council set a new internal exchange rate of U.S.$1 = RMB 2.8, applicable to all visible foreign trade activities (except tourism), with the objective of increasing export performance* while discouraging unnecessary imports of expensive capital equipment. Prior to the new decentralization policies, such decisions could be made directly in Beijing, but many enterprises now make their own decisions, which can be influenced only indirectly.

Reaction from outside China was that this amounted to actual devaluation or only a temporary way station in that direction. The GAEC pointedly denied any "possibility of a devaluation of renminbi. Talk of a dual exchange rate [was] utterly groundless."[38] It insisted that there was "only one exchange rate" and that the second "rate" was for the "internal settlement of accounts" merely designed to subsidize exporters. Reportedly, the new system had not been discussed with the IMF, although Article 4.1 of the IMF's Articles of Agreement requires members to provide the fund with an explanation of changes that occur in a country's exchange system.[39] There have been some reports that the split rate was in existence in the 1960s and mid-1970s via a foreign exchange "surcharge." A senior and well-informed official denied this to the author, stating that the system had not been used before.

One major difficulty with an official devaluation of RMB would be the effect on existing and future deposits made by foreigners through overseas offices of the BOC. Hundreds of millions of dollars in hard currencies have been attracted into RMB accounts since 1970, particularly through Hong Kong; much of this was attracted on the basis of advertisements about the stability of RMB and "the absence of the danger of devaluation." The problem is not insurmountable. Such accounts vary, and at least some were offered

---

*Exports would not be cheapter, but export income would produce higher RMB profits for the Chinese enterprise. This has caused some U.S. importers to renegotiate their price, arguing with their Chinese supplier that, since every dollar will earn more RMB, export prices should be lowered to increase overall volume.

with the option of withdrawal at the rate of conversion prevailing at the time of original deposit or that prevailing at the time of withdrawal. Other accounts could be dealt with by a one-time-only percentage increase in the RMB deposit equal to the percentage of devaluation.

If China were to officially devalue its currency, one effect would be to aggravate inflationary pressure; this would occur because of the massive commitments to import grains and cotton staples, whose purchase cannot be deferred as readily as steel plants. In addition, lower prices would lead to a decline in tourism income, because the increased demand generated by lower prices cannot be met owing to hotel shortages. There would also be an immediate loss of income for exports made under long-term, fixed-price contracts.

New Exchange Control Regulations and Markets

With trade and travel centrally controlled until recent years, China has been able to enforce a strict set of exchange controls. All foreign exchange holdings within the country were to be deposited with the BOC and were withdrawable only upon conversion into domestic currency at fixed exchange rates. Most foreign currency entered the country in one of two ways: bank transfers to Foreign Trade Corporations and bank transfers or cash by post from overseas Chinese. Both methods were easily regulated.

Relaxation of travel restrictions and decentralization of trade coincided with relaxation in exchange controls in 1978. As a consequence, some illegal currency trading began, a fact that greatly concerned policy makers and contributed to reimposition of strict controls.

New foreign exchange controls were issued by the State Council on December 18, 1980, and became effective on March 1, 1981 (see Appendix B).[40] While quite detailed and useful in clarifying many points raised by traders and potential investors, they were not in themselves complete. They referred internally to detailed enforcement provisions yet to be announced, regulations for special economic zones and border trade to be formulated by concerned provincial and municipal governments, as well as examining and approval procedures for foreign loans.

The new regulations cover foreign exchange in its broadest terms. Article 2 defines this to include currencies, as well as securities and financial instruments denominated in foreign currency, such as bonds, bills, drafts, and bank deposit certificates. Administration is generally, but not completely, centralized in the GAEC, which is directly appointed by the State Council.[41] The GAEC is represented locally throughout China by its branch offices, which are in the same buildings as the BOC branches. The BOC is appointed as the executive agency through which all foreign exchange must be bought and sold unless otherwise expressly exempted. Foreign exchange may be possessed only with GAEC approval. The State Council has retained for itself the power to approve the issue of foreign-currency-denominated securities. The GAEC shares jurisdiction with the FIC and the State Council over planned foreign borrowing by banks or enterprises. Despite these shared powers, exchange controls appear to be broadly centralized under the GAEC.

In general, it is an offense to retain in possession, circulate, use, mortgage, assign, or deposit abroad any foreign exchange except by or through the BOC. The rules apply to individuals, enterprises, state bodies, joint ventures, and to enterprises permitted to retain or control a portion of their foreign exchange receipts. These later portions and all other permitted holdings (for example, through a loan authorized under the National Development Plan) must be placed in foreign currency accounts with the BOC. Two accounts are available for state or collective organizations: a quota account for currency allocated to the organization under the current plan and a deposit account for foreign exchange earnings or proceeds of borrowings. All enterprises, except registered state-owned FTCs, need a license from the local foreign trade bureau of the Export Affairs Administration Commission before they can trade or hold foreign exchange. This license is in addition to approval of the GAEC.

Joint ventures and other enterprises with foreign investment are subject to more relaxed rules.[42] While all their foreign exchange receipts must be deposited with, and payments go through, the BOC, no prior approval of the GAEC seems required. Periodic reports are required, and permission must be obtained before a domestic payment or receipt may be made in any currency other than RMB. Net profits are freely remittable as are all "other legitimate earnings" (for example, royalty payments or license fees), but remittal of foreign capital must go through the GAEC, as must assets upon liquidation.

Article 10 is indicative of the problems caused by sudden decentralization in 1979, under which numerous regional government agencies and state enterprises entered into their own arrangements for foreign exchange commitments or borrowings. The central state-planning authorities had no idea how much foreign exchange was being committed or obtained, or if totals were within the current plan goals. From March 1, 1981, it seems that banks handling all import and export transactions are to check whether receipt or payment is authorized. This reintroduces an important check against abuse of authority, as well as enabling better accounting of trade statistics.

Chapter 3 of the regulations deals with individuals and permits residents to retain control of certain percentages of existing foreign exchange holdings brought into China by persons taking up permanent residence or holdings remitted to residents. These retained percentages must, however, be deposited with the BOC and may be remitted or taken back out of China. The regulations do not say so, but presumably the depositor must bear the exchange risk on these forced deposits, unless the BOC will accept such funds into foreign-currency-denominated accounts. Overseas Chinese and foreign nationals entering China for a short stay (including consultants, teachers, students, technicians, or staff/workers) may keep, remit, deposit, or take out foreign exchange.

Detailed provisions for enforcement were to be formulated, but the December 1980 regulations proscribe punishments of fines, confiscation, imprisonment, and "compulsory exchange of the foreign currency." In this regard it should be noted that, under the 1979 Criminal Code effective January 1, 1980, a minimum three-year sentence is set for "any foreigner who has committed a crime against China."[43] In particular, the Criminal Code contains a section dealing with "crimes against the socialist economic order," which includes exchange-control violations, and under which some Hong Kong businessmen were convicted in 1979 and 1980. Customs and currency violations can lead to a term of from three to ten years imprisonment.

In an effort to counter the small, but growing, black market in foreign exchange, special foreign-currency certificates have been issued to foreigners since 1980.[44] The new regulations do not mention or abolish these certificates, although their abolishment had been rumored in late 1980. The certificates do not appear incompatible with the regulations, and their demise cannot automatically be assumed.

The external parity of RMB remains a unilateral decision of the GAEC and the BOC, even though a limited free market for foreign exchange exists at various BOC branches.[45] At these branches, companies that possess foreign exchange authorized to be spent under their quota may instead offer to sell it to a bidder through the BOC. Reportedly, no official rate is set, market forces being allowed to operate. The differentials are substantial. For example, during May 1981, while the official external rate against the dollar was RMB 1.5 = U.S.$1, the domestic rate was RMB 2.8 = U.S.$1, and free market rates were as high as RMB 3.36 = U.S.$1. The buyer must, of course, already be authorized to spend the foreign exchange it purchases. The market was initiated either because the BOC did not have as much foreign exchange as the quotas authorized or it did not have it available at the time all enterprises desired funds. By going to the market, enterprises willing to pay premiums over the official rate can try to purchase exchange as and when they need it.

GENERAL STRUCTURE OF CHINA'S BANKING SYSTEM

The People's Bank of China

The People's Republic of China was proclaimed on October 1, 1949, and virtually all of China's banking system was then consolidated into one institution, the People's Bank of China, which had been founded a year earlier. Today the PBOC still functions as both China's central bank and its main commercial banking system.[46] Although the banking system has been reformed and new banks have been created, the PBOC remains at the hub of China's banking system and continues to play a central role in the planning and supervision of National Development Plans. The PBOC issues currency, is the center of the settlement in the economy, maintains savings accounts for individuals and entities, provides credit to commercial enterprises, controls the money supply, and represents the State Treasury.

In July 1978, Wu Chui-Li, chief of the State Planning Commission, announced to the National Conference on Finance and Trade that the bank would have a new elevated position of unprecedented power.[47] This followed on the footsteps of the National People's Congress of March 1978, where it had emerged that the bank's new president, Li Baohua, had also been made a minister in the State Council. The bank's importance and independence was thus confirmed, as its direct relationship to the State Council makes it akin to a special agency of the government or a cabinet ministry. The only other financial body headed up by a member of the State Council is the Ministry of Finance itself. Its combined structure as both a state organ and an economic department gives it considerable power.

Structure and Personnel

The PBOC is headquartered in Beijing and shares the building used by the Ministry of Finance. The bank has 20 branches, one for each province and autonomous municipality, with a further 218 so-called central subbranches at the district level of government, and 2,220 at the county level. It recently gave the total number of its offices throughout the nation as over 37,000.

The PBOC reports a staff of 330,000, of whom 1,200 work in the head office in Beijing. As of late 1981 Li Baohua remained president and Shang Ming was senior vice-president. Observers of the bank appear to agree that the caliber of its senior staff is very high. They are described as solid, professional career personnel with experience in a number of economic posts. Although today the bank is criticized, along with all other institutions, in the drive toward modernization, its high status within the country is confirmed by the success with which the staff weathered the storm of the Cultural Revolution.[48]

While the supervisory role of bankers was reduced in the recent past, the PBOC's management role in the economy is currently being revived and strengthened. Chinese bankers were cut off from modern banking practices for a long time. As a consequence they are short of trained staff to take on the new roles being assigned to them. In most branches approximately one-half of the staff are cashiers and bookkeepers, one-quarter are credit officers, and the remainder are officials, planners, and service staff. These cashiers, bookkeepers, credit officers, and planners, while having capacity and senior management of great ability, are relatively unsophisticated and somewhat lacking in familiarity with newer types of banking transactions and terminology. This may in part account for China's reluctance to accept Western legal requirements for syndicated loans when first offered to China during 1978-79. The problem of staff training is recognized by the Chinese themselves. Official press reports have cited examples of uncollected loans, embezzlement, and improper supervision of construction by bank officials with the comment that "the efficiency of our banks . . . trails far behind banks in other parts of the world."[49] With this aspect of Chinese society being modernized, corresponding attention and resources are being channeled into upgrading of staff.

Functions and Operations

The People's Bank of China has at least three main functions. It is both China's central bank and its main commercial bank, but its most important and distinctive function is supervising China's National Development Plans to ensure that they are being properly carried out.

As a central bank it is charged with the following duties: issuing currency, maintaining the accounts of state enterprises, controlling credit and money supply, and regulating foreign bank operations inside China. Under its supervision (or what Chinese bankers now prefer to call "leadership") the BOC operates the foreign exchange and reserve accounts of China, and the Bank of Agriculture provides banking services in rural areas.

The PBOC, while exercising control over the money supply, also serves as the center of credit. All transactions between enterprises with a value over RMB 30 must be conducted through the banking system. This ensures that, apart from consumer spending on retail purchases, the money supply consists entirely of bank accounts.

The PBOC is the centralized and monopolistic retail bank of a centrally planned economy. It has an additional and unfamiliar function compared with its Western counterparts, as it is charged with supervising the fulfillment of National Development Plan goals. By handling all payments of state enterprises it can simultaneously scrutinize their performance and activities.[50] It is the PBOC's credit officers at provincial and district levels who are supposed to ensure that financial requests conform with the National Development Plan; they also visit enterprises to inspect accounts and operations. Through daily contact with industry and enterprise management, the PBOC can push these institutions to maximize their profitability, export earnings, and domestic production.

With its recently upgraded status and power, the bank will play a commanding role in the monitoring of the nation's industrial performance. The task is to be carried out through financial and economic discipline rather than Communist dogma. A People's Daily editorial stated that "the banks should support those enterprises that fulfill state plans and have effective management. They should withhold loans from those [enterprises] where management is bad and no progress is being made."[51] It is too early to see how effective implementation of the new push has been, especially at the provincial level. The large national deficits caused by unauthorized overspending indicate the need to implement real controls.

Bank of Agriculture

The Agricultural Bank of China or Bank of Agriculture was first established in 1955, shortly after the Revolution, and was closed down for the first time only a few years thereafter in 1957.[52] Reopened in 1963, or 1965, it was closed again during the Cultural Revolution. Its most recent rebirth was 14 years later in the spring of 1979, when the PBOC's rural offices and agricultural credit functions were separated from it. This latest revival serves two purposes: it is part of a larger effort to boost agricultural production, and it helps put an end to alleged abuses of bank loans by peasants and village officials. Bank officials, attending the first national conference after the 1979 revival, adopted as their central task the accumulation of "more funds for People's communes, production brigades and state-owned agricultural enterprises" in order that "local resources can be tapped and agricultural growth and modernization speeded up."[53]

The bank functions under the direct control of the State Council, but the PBOC has general policy powers of supervision and acts as the coordinator between the Bank of Agriculture and the rest of the banking system.[54] The bank is headed by Fang Gao, whose headquarters staff numbers at least 200, with a general staff of approximately 200,000 distributed among 3,000 branches and 30,000 commune offices.

Bank of China

The Bank of China is that country's international banking institution, with origins that can be traced back to a private bank in the early 1900s. Reorganized into a "State Bank" in 1912 during the Republic of China period, the Kuomintang government took over one-half of the equity in 1935. After the Revolution (1950) the People's Bank of China took over the state's share of the equity, thereby increasing it to two-thirds, and reorganized the BOC as a subsidiary of the PBOC. The new government continued its nominally separate existence to facilitate China's claims to Nationalist investments abroad and to retain the established commercial goodwill of this Nationalist banking institution. Until very recently it was a joint state-private enterprise with nominal private shareholders.

The orignal private shareholders were allowed to continue their participation, and technically an element of private ownership existed until 1981. In its 1962 Articles of Association the BOC was referred to as a "State and private jointly-owned corporation with limited liability." This was confirmed in a 1980 interview that this author had with a local BOC official in Guangzhou who was formerly involved in dispersal of dividend checks to local private shareholders. No market in the bank's stock existed, so new private investment was impossible. The long-standing element of private and capitalist ownership was interesting, but for some time it was clear that the bank operated only under direct government supervision and the leadership of the PBOC.

The head of the bank is a member of the State Council, so the bank enjoys the rank of a separate cabinet position and, as stated, has been under the direct authority of the State Council since 1979. At the end of 1980 the president was Bu-Ming and the honorary chairman was Oioo Peixin, who retains his senior position with the PBOC.

The bank's functions have recently expanded, and it is now responsible for supervising the "unified management of China's foreign exchange business, the international clearance of all commercial and noncommercial exchange, the organization of foreign funds in a planned way and the handling of import and export credit loans."[55] The BOC still implements policies concerning overseas Chinese affairs and remittances with the obvious aim of increasing remittances and other noncommercial foreign exchange income.

Bank of Construction

The People's Bank of Construction or Construction Bank was first organized in October 1954 and charged with the allocation of funds budgeted for long-term capital investments and for some short-term investments. Its capital construction duties were transferred to it from the Bank of Communications. Its means of financing were bank credit created on its own, the idle balance of funds appropriated to it, and, most important, short-term loans from the PBOC. Ceasing to function in 1966, its staff was absorbed by the PBOC. The bank has been reactivated since at least early 1977 (although only formally proclaimed in 1979) and now operates through 2,500 branches nationwide.[56]

While operating under the direct authority of the State Council since November 1979, day-to-day work is supervised by the Ministry of Finance (MOF) as well as the Capital Construction Commission.[57] The MOF most closely controls the bank and is the main source of its funds. Responsibilities include the following: allocating funds and extending loans for capital construction and the renovation, expansion, and rebuilding of existing enterprises; and overseeing the expenditures of funds budgeted to capital construction.[58] The bank itself was ordered by a 1979 national party conference to supervise all major industrial, transportation, communications, agricultural, forestry, commercial, and tourism projects for a one-year trial period. Under the "Trial Regulations for Granting Capital Construction Loans" each project is to be governed by a written contract whose terms must be followed. If the terms are broken, the borrowing enterprise's loan accelerates and further credit is to be denied. Interest is to be charged, and heavy industry may repay within 15 years. The bank has the power to withdraw funds from a defaulting enterprise's ordinary operational accounts in order to repay capital loans.[59] The government hopes that the bank will play an active role in cutting down on waste and inefficiency and that the bank's loans (believed to carry a 3 percent interest charge) will gradually replace direct government appropriations for future capital-investment projects.

One can see that the exact role of banks in the economy is presently experimental; however, the present position is that long-term credit supervision is done by the Construction Bank, while the People's Bank controls practically all short-term funds. The Construction Bank's enlarged tasks were the result of recent successes. The Chinese press reported that the Construction Bank saved the state budget the equivalent of U.S.$1 billion through its efficient management of capital projects. A further U.S.$500 million was saved by enforcement of state directives on the allocation of funds. Its initial policy is to give priority to light and textile industries, enterprises that produce export commodities and require relatively small investments, but which yield quick returns and turn out products urgently needed on the market.[60] Relative to foreign trade, the bank will give priority to enterprises importing foreign equipment to boost production, to conduct compensation trade with foreign countries, to process raw materials from abroad on order, to fulfill requirements under approved joint ventures, and to fulfill overseas construction contracts. The bank's task is immense. In an economy the size of China's it is not surprising that "capital construction" in 1979 totaled RMB 41.8 billion—up 17.4 percent from 1978.[61] The national government's share was RMB 39.5 billion, of which the Bank of Construction would be responsible for the major portion.

General Administration of Exchange Control

Owing to the overwhelming importance of foreign exchange in the modernization effort, the Chinese government established a new organization to control China's foreign exchange transactions in early 1979. The General Administration of Exchange Control is linked, but subordinate to, the PBOC and is charged with supervising the BOC.[62] The establishment of this institution signifies the central government's recognition of the need for close supervision of foreign exchange and a decision that the task can no longer be left to bankers alone.

The GAEC took over existing control regulations but was empowered to issue new exchange controls; it did this in late 1980. The GAEC supervises all functions connected with the balance of payments. In theory, the GAEC is separate from the banking institutions and reports directly to the State Council. Since 1979 the GAEC's approval is required when state enterprises and foreign trade corporations make credit arrangements for foreign exchange (that is, foreign loans). Foreign currency credits and guarantees are, therefore, centrally controlled.

At the time of this writing, the distinction between the GAEC and the BOC is difficult to determine. Both are headquartered in the same building and share common staff. Bu-Ming presided over both organizations in late 1980. GAEC branch activities are carried out through BOC branches in the larger cities and ports, presumably by BOC branch staff seconded to the GAEC. The author was told by BOC officials that their staff "will actually carry out most of the tasks assigned to the [GAEC]."

The organization of Beijing headquarters is in three departments: planning, exchange control, and exchange rates. The first is charged with planning foreign exchange policies and coordinating the nation's exchange earnings with the competing demands for exchange allocations or borrowings. In this role the GAEC appears to resemble a planning committee of the board of directors of a major corporation: the State Council. The second department drafts and oversees enforcement of exchange-control regulations. These two departments have a headquarters staff of 10 people each. The third department is described by the GAEC itself as working with the PBOC and the BOC in setting China's foreign exchange rates. The BOC, however, maintains that the exchange rate is set by a formula established by the State Council, which it alone applies without the daily permission of the GAEC and the PBOC. In this role the GAEC is subordinated to the PBOC, which must approve the rates proposed by its staff. Given the tremendous range and rate of change in the nation's foreign banking system, the GAEC's role can be expected to undergo significant evolution in the coming years.

Ministry of Finance

An overview of China's domestic or international banking systems must include the Ministry of Finance because of its role as a source of banking funds and its authority over capital construction finance. The latter task places it in direct link with the World Bank. The minister of finance, Wu Bo, was named as China's governor to the World Bank, and Vice-Minister Li Peng was named alternate.

Capital Construction Commission

The Capital Construction Commission (CCC) affects banking through its regulatory role. Originally begun in 1958, abolished in 1961, and replaced by the State Planning Commission, the CCC was reestablished in 1975. In 1980 it was headed by Gu Mu, who also headed the Foreign Investment Commission and the Import-Export Commission. Not much is known about its staff or structure, but it must approve all major state capital-construction projects, including those seeking loans from the Construction Bank.

China International Trust and Investment Corporation

The China International Trust and Investment Corporation (CITIC) is the newest financial institution and was formed as a joint state-private corporation with nominal private ownership. The board of directors includes several foreign members, among them some of Hong Kong's best-known Chinese businessmen. It is not discussed in detail because its banking functions and interworking with other Chinese banks are very limited. Its functions are to invest (or hold in trust for investment) in joint venture companies involving foreign capital. The CITIC may also invest foreign funds in wholly Chinese-owned companies involved in exporting. The CITIC is in part modeled upon the state Overseas Chinese Investment Company and its provincial counterparts. These operated from about 1952 to 1964 and were established to attract foreign exchange from overseas Chinese for investment in industry. The investor retained ownership of the funds and was repaid after a 12-year term. A dividend of 8 percent per annum was paid and was remittable outside China to a maximum of 50 percent of dividends paid in the year in question. These companies were, like the CITIC, originally joint state-private companies but were reorganized into state companies in 1957.

RELATIONSHIP OF INSTITUTIONS

With the introduction of CCC and CITIC it is now possible to diagram the banking system and its interrelationships (see Figure 1). At the top is the State Council, which exercises control centrally and directly through cabinet decision making; the heads of major banks and financial institutions are members of the council. Control is also exercised indirectly through the difficult-to-grasp concept of "guidance and leadership." No doubt day-to-day decision making is internal. Policy guidance flows through the People's Bank, and major policy is made and directly enforced at the State Council level.

In Figure 1 it appears that the MOF is only on equal footing with several institutions. As stated, these banks, except the PBOC are only somewhat like ministries. All these institutions are, however, dwarfed in size and influence when compared with the MOF. Aside from the obvious tendency for senior staff to interchange and thus have indirect influence, the ministry also exerts a powerful and direct influence over the policies and procedures of the banking institutions.

FIGURE 1

China's National Banking and Financial System

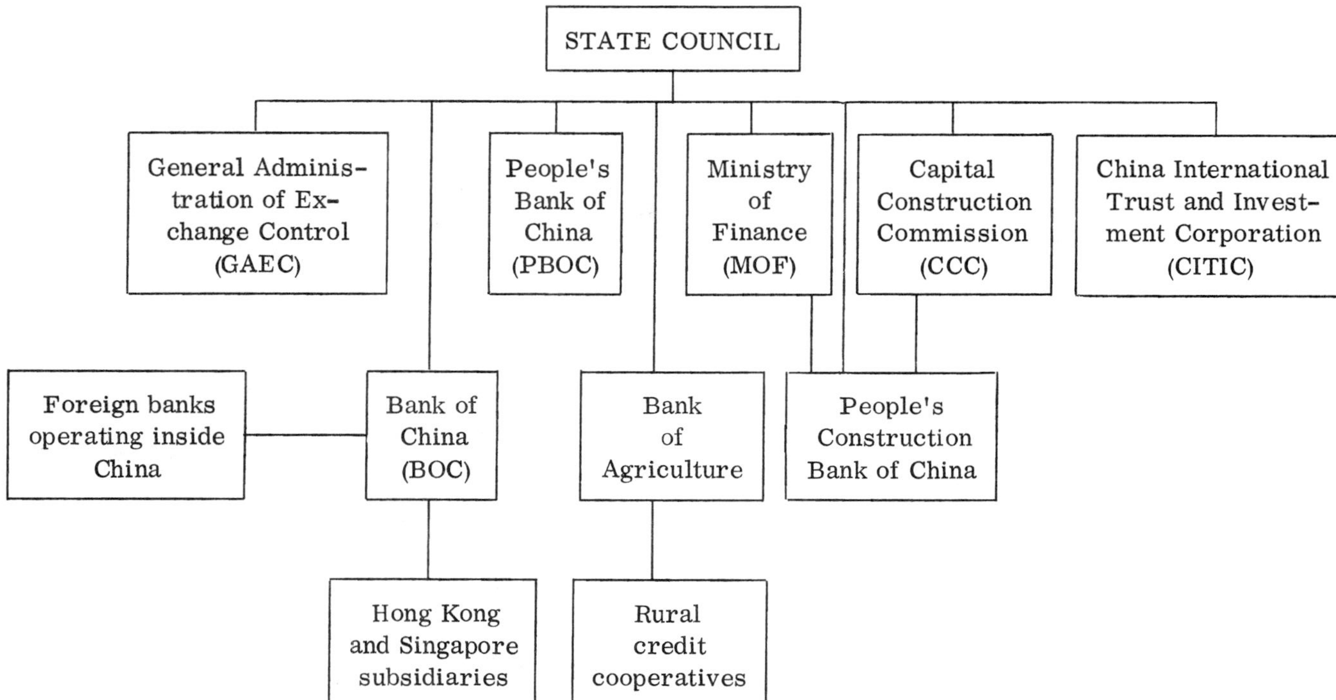

The BOC's Hong Kong and Singapore subsidiaries are outlined in Chapter 2. From Figure 1 the complex controls over the BOC are apparent. Directly under the State Council, it is theoretically equal to the PBOC, yet it is subject to the "leadership" of both the PBOC and the GAEC. Similarly, the Bank of Construction is directly linked to the State Council, as well as the Capital Construction Commission and the Ministry of Finance. Finally, the GAEC is somewhat subordinate to the PBOC and directs the BOC, especially in regulations and rates for foreign exchange.

The PBOC, for many years virtually a monopoly banking institution, has found its power and functions diluted since 1978. The changes cannot have uniformly pleased senior management, yet it is impossible to know whether the changes have occurred because the pragmatic post-Mao government felt that new specialized institutions would be more efficient. The government may have been motivated by political motives or displeasure over the way the PBOC used its authority. Nevertheless, the PBOC has retained extensive authority over the Bank of Agriculture, the BOC, and the GAEC.

The promotion of the banking system came during a period when many of China's financial specialists were lamenting the traditional practices of allocating investment funds on a grant basis. Waste and inefficiency were encouraged by unconditional interest-free loans. Cancellation or nonenforcement of repayment obligations often transformed loans into grants. The People's Daily complained that "the results are expansion of capital construction, slow progress, high cost, and substantial waste."[63] Several reforms were needed, most of which have been outlined.

The rising influence and power of banks and banking practices was a much-needed and long-expected aspect of modernization. A pragmatic approach to financing is logically part of, and essential to, the present leadership's plans for economic growth. However, prospects for successful implementation must be viewed with caution. The decision to shift from government grants for capital requirements to interest-bearing loans will not be easy. It was taken after barely one year's experimenting in only some of the provinces. Many inefficient producers are unlikely to survive on the new financial diet. For many concerns, pricing and accounting, as well as allocation of resources, are simply not geared to, nor can they easily be structured to, the repayment of loans.[64] Given the relative lack of commercial banking experiences at the provincial level and the shortage of staff trained in credit analysis or otherwise competent to evaluate loan applications, the shift of responsibility onto the shoulders of banks will also be stress filled.

NOTES

1. Audrey Donnithorne, "Aspects of Neo-Liuist Economic Policy," Australian Journal of Chinese Affairs 3 (1980): 27-39.

2. The author has relied heavily on Audrey Donnithorne, China's Economic System (New York: Frederick A. Praeger, 1967), which is to be revised in late 1981. The Joint Economic Committee of the U.S. Congress will also have published its new study of China's economy by early 1982.

3. Details were covered extensively throughout the 1978 and 1979 issues of all leading journals of contemporary Chinese studies. Business readers will find the coverage in China Business Review and Japan's China Trade Report most helpful.

4. Paul G. Hare, "China's System of Economic Planning," mimeographed (University of Sterling, 1980).

5. Colina MacDougall, "China Learns from East Europe's Economic Reforms," Financial Times, November 14, 1980, p. 31, states that this is China's third round at decentralization and sketches the participants in previous attempts.

6. Paul D. Reynolds, "Doing Business with the People's Republic of China: Tax Considerations," International Lawyer 14 (1980): 49-72.

7. Pauline Loong, "Capitalizing on New-Socialism," Far Eastern Economic Review, August 15, 1980, pp. 40-42.

8. Gordon Bennett, "The Emerging Business Climate," East Asian Executive Reports 2 (March 1980): 3, 15-16.

9. The philosophy of Soviet monetary theory and the Chinese adaptation are outlined by Cheng Chü-yuan, Monetary Affairs of Communist China, Communist China Problem Research Series (Hong Kong: Union Research Institute, 1954), pp. 1-8, 44-48. For purposes of comparison a brief description of modern prerevolutionary China's monetary system may be found in George Allen and Audrey Donnithorne, Western Enterprise in Far Eastern Economic Development: China and Japan (London: Macmillan, 1954), pp. 102-19. See also Katharine Huang Hsiao, Money and Monetary Policy in Communist China (New York: Columbia University Press, 1971).

10. The goals are discussed at length by Gordon Bennett, China's Finance and Trade (New York: Sharpe, 1978), pp. 137-46.

11. Associated Press news report from Shanghai, October 18, 1948, cited in Tadoa Miyashita, The Currency and Financial System of Mainland China, trans. T. R. McEwan (Seattle: University of Washington Press, 1966), p. 58.

12. Miyashita, Currency and Financial System, pp. 1-54.

13. Ibid., pp. 59-60. On the role of commodities as backing for Chinese currency, see Li Hsien-nien, "Some Problems in the Practical Aspects of Financial Administration and Credit Provision," Hung Chi [Red flag] 1 (1960): 10-12; Huang Ta, "The Principles Governing Bank Loans and Their Relation to Currency Circulation," Ching Chi Yenchiu [Economic research], no. 9 (1962); and Lin Chi-k'en, "On the Operation of the Laws Governing Currency Circulation under a Socialist System," Ching Chi Yenchiu [Economic research] no. 2 (1963).

14. In writing this section I am indebted far more than the notes would indicate to the following more detailed sources: Fred C. Hung, "The Role of Money and Credit in Communist China's Economic Planning," in East Asian Occasional Papers, vol. 1, ed. Harry Lamley (Honolulu: University of Hawaii, 1969); S. C. Tsiang, "Money and Banking in Communist China," in An Economic Profile of Mainland China, vol. 1, ed. U.S., Congress, Joint Economic Committee (Washington, D.C.: Government Printing Office, 1967), pp. 323-39; Cheng Chü-yuan, Monetary Affairs; and Bennett, China's Finance.

15. Chi Ts'ai-ch'eng, Concise Treatise on Comprehensive Financial Planning (Beijing: People's Republic of China, 1961), p. 29.

16. Pierre-Henri Cassou, "The Chinese Monetary System," Chinese Economic Studies 9 (1975-76): 82-97, reprinted in China Quarterly 59, July-September 1974, pp. 559-66; L. Mulkern, "The Financial Aspects of China Trade," in Trade with China, ed. American Management Association (New York: AMA, 1972), p. 19; and Dick Wilson, "How Banks Work in China," Banker 130 (January 1980): 19-27.

17. Tsiang, "Money and Banking," p. 337.

18. Yang Po, "New China's Policy," Peking Review, November 20, 1964.

19. Miyashita, Currency and Financial System, p. 137. Translated extracts may be found in Chao, ed., Economic Planning and Organization in Mainland China, vol. 1 (Cambridge, Mass.: Harvard Center for East-Asian Studies, 1959), pp. 255-57, which contains translations of many other early financial laws.

20. Hung, "Role of Money," pp. 58, 66; quoting People's Bank of China, Problems of Materialism in the Works of the People's Bank of China (Peking: People's Republic of China, 1955), p. 42.

21. Dwight Perkins, Market Control and Planning in Communist China (Cambridge, Mass.: Harvard University Press, 1966), p. 126.

22. Hung, "Role of Money," pp. 51-59. Professor Bennett explains that the general approach was to "decentralize as many planning decisions as possible to provincial or local levels and then" try to balance matters. Bennett, China's Finance, p. 142.

23. Bennett, China's Finance, p. 141.

24. Alexander Eckstein, China's Economic Revolution (New York: Cambridge University Press, 1977), p. 167.

25. Xinhua News Agency release, February 9, 1980; People's Daily, February 8, 1980; and Beijing Review, April 14, 1980, p. 5. The inflation rate had reached 6 percent per annum by April 1980. Financial Times, May 1, 1980, p. 3.

26. Martin Bailey, "Chinese Aid in Action," in Chinese Road to Development, 2d ed., ed. Neville Maxwell (London: Pergamon, 1979), pp. 289-97; and John F. Cooper, China's Foreign Aid in 1978 (Washington, D.C.: American Enterprise Institute for Foreign Policy Research, 1979), pp. 1-2, 42.

27. Nicolas Wolfers, "Financing the China Trade," in Trading with China, ed. Colina MacDougall (London: McGraw-Hill, 1980), pp. 95-117.

28. Audrey Donnithorne, China's Economic System, p. 418.

29. See James Stepanek, "Beijing's Continuing Retrenchment," China Business Review 8 (January-February 1981): 16.

30. This section is largely based on information in Frank Münzel, "Ways of Payment in Foreign Trade," in Law and Politics in China's Foreign Trade, ed. Victor Li (Seattle: University of Washington Press, 1977), pp. 270-86.

31. See Charles F. Remer, The Trade Agreements of Communist China, RAND Paper no. 2208, Washington, D.C., 1961, p. 40.

32. Published in U.S.-China Business Review 2 (July-August 1975): 55.

33. See, generally, Alistair Wrightman, "How Japan Finances Trade with China," U.S.-China Business Review 2 (March-April 1975): 30-34.

34. Barry Kramer, "People's Banker," Wall Street Journal, December 1, 1976, p. 1, col. 1.

35. For an older study, see James Stepanek, "How Are China's Exchange Rates Set?" U.S.-China Business Review 3 (January-February 1976): 11; and David Denny, "International Finance in the People's Republic of China," in China: A Reassessment of the Economy, ed. U.S., Congress, Joint Economic Committee (Washington, D.C.: Government Printing Office, 1975), p. 664.

36. Ibid.

37. Far Eastern Economic Report, December 12, 1980, p. 62.

38. The fact that the GAEC, not the BOC, replied to press comments may well be quite significant. If the BOC sets the exchange rate, as it appears to assert, why was the GAEC the spokesman? It could either be explained by recognizing the GAEC's policy-making role, or in that the BOC felt it would have been inappropriate for it to reply to press comment. Xinhua News Agency release, December 15, 1980.

39. James Stepanek, "Beijing's Continuing Retrenchment," p. 18.

40. "The Provisional Regulations for Exchange Control of the People's Republic of China," unofficial trans. in Beijing Review, January 26, 1981, pp. 25-28 (reproduced as Appendix B).

41. See text accompanying notes 62-64 below. The relationship between these organizations and other financial institutions is summarized in "China's Financial Institutions," China Business Review 7 (July-August 1980): 15-18. The GAEC has recently restructured its goals and priorities. Xinhua News Agency release, January 13, 1981.

42. This policy is confirmed in Beijing Review, January 26, 1981, p. 6, where the reason given for relaxed treatment is to encourage investment from abroad.

43. See Asian Wall Street Journal Weekly, February 11, 1980.

44. Developments leading up to the ban on use of foreign currency and the issuance of certificates are described in Wall Street Journal, October 3, 1979, p. 16; Wall Street Journal, January 28, 1980, p. 10; and New York Times, February 17, 1980, p. 13.

45. Pauline Loong, "Have Dollars Will Sell," Far Eastern Economic Review, January 9, 1981, pp. 53-54. But see update and correction in Afterword.

46. Cassou, "Chinese Monetary System," pp. 82-97, reprinted in China Quarterly 59 (July-September 1974): 559-66; and China's Financial Institutions," China Business Review 7 (July-August 1980): 15-18.

47. "A New Capitalist Role for the People's Bank," Business Week, September 11, 1978, p. 740.

48. Dick Wilson, "The Bank of China Steps Out," Banker 124 (February 1974): 105-10.

49. Wall Street Journal, May 8, 1979, p. 40, col. 1. See also Jerome Cohen, "Is There Law in China?" International Trade Law Journal 5 (1979): 73-86.

50. Huang Hsiao, Money and Monetary Policy, p. 15.

51. Wall Street Journal, May 8, 1979, p. 40, col. 1. See also the detailed account in "The People's Bank," Wall Street Journal, January 8, 1982, p. 1.

52. "China's Financial Institutions" gives the dates as 1951-55.

53. Xinhua News Agency release, October 23, 1979.

54. Statistics and details in this paragraph were supplied by the bank to China Business Review 7 (July-August 1980): 16.

55. Melinda Liu, "China Will Stay Cautious Despite a U.S.$60 Billion Credit," Far Eastern Economic Review, October 5, 1979, p. 75.

56. See, generally, Hsiao, Money and Monetary Policy, p. 33; and Hung, "Role of Money," p. 54.

57. Xinhua News Agency release, November 26, 1979.

58. Beijing Review, December 21, 1979, p. 8, citing Xinhua News Agency release, December 5, 1979.

59. Beijing Review, December 7, 1979, pp. 4-5.

60. Ibid., December 21, 1979, p. 8.

61. Ibid., May 19, 1980, p. 12.

62. Interview by the author of BOC officials, December 1979; Wall Street Journal, April 13, 1979, p. 15, col. 5; and Leo Goodstadt, "Peking Elevates the Bank of China's Status," Euromoney, September 1979, pp. 66-70.

63. Goodstadt, "Peking Elevates the Bank," pp. 66, 70.

64. International Herald Tribune, September 2, 1980.

2

THE FOREIGN BANKING SYSTEM

BANK OF CHINA

The Bank of China (BOC) is a wholly state-owned corporation with a separate legal identity. After the Revolution the bank was originally reestablished as a joint state-private enterprise with nominal private shareholders and subordinate to the People's Bank of China (PBOC), for whom it acted as agent in handling foreign exchange and international settlements. Operating today under direct legal authority of the State Council, it is the sole foreign exchange bank for China. It carries on central bank functions in relation to international settlements, shares control of foreign exchange transactions, and executes needed international money transfers. Its domestic operations are, thus, essentially limited to foreign exchange banking. This is in contrast with its overseas operations, which, as will be seen, are broader. Overseas, the BOC offers the whole range of banking business: retail, commercial, and merchant banking aimed at local markets where the branches operate. The BOC's relationship to other banks was set out in the previous chapter.

In the past, as well as the present, China has had foreign-currency cash-flow problems, because the Ministry of Foreign

Trade and numerous state enterprises were able to make foreign exchange commitments on their own authority. When the Bank of China attempted to intervene, these enterprises insisted that the bank go through the PBOC and then to the State Council. However, with recent changes in the banking system's structure, the BOC works directly with the State Council and the General Administration of Exchange Control (GAEC) in planning and allocating foreign exchange commitments, although the PBOC retains day-to-day supervision of BOC work. The new arrangement also constitutes State Council recognition of its need for professional banking advice.[1] The State Council will now be able to regulate the official financial guarantees granted by government agencies to foreigners—particularly bankers. All such guarantees on the national level will come from the Bank of China and not from state bodies, whose legal authority to issue such guarantees was questionable and unregulated.[2]

The BOC's impact on the domestic money supply is negligible, because it is limited to the conversion of private holdings of foreign exchange into Chinese currency. The law requires all foreign exchange holdings within the country (with limited exemptions for overseas visitors to China) to be deposited with the BOC. Such deposits may only be withdrawn upon conversion into domestic currency at a fixed exchange rate. Most such private holdings come into the bank through overseas remittances. With the recent increase in tourism, large amounts of cash, foreign exchange, and traveler's checks are being received by the bank. The BOC imposes tight control over renminbi (RMB) purchases and sales. In general all spot or forward purchases of RMB by purchasers outside China must be backed by reference to a specific contract with a Chinese foreign-trade corporation or government enterprise.[3] The spot and forward exchange market rates are fixed periodically by the GAEC and the BOC and are adjusted from time to time.[4] The bank purchases all of China's official foreign exchange earnings, as well as sells foreign exchange to enterprises and government agencies. Purchasers inside China may now buy foreign currency on rudimentary exchange markets, as long as the amount is within their authorized foreign exchange quota. These markets were described in Chapter 1.

The BOC works closely with the other major state trading institutions, including the China Council for Promotion of International Trade and the Foreign Trade Corporations. These latter institutions are subject to common controlling authority by the State Council and are guided by the Ministry of Foreign Trade. It has been common in the past for these institutions and the BOC to exchange personnel, especially between the Ministry of Foreign Trade and the China Council for Promotion of International Trade.[5]

China has structured its trade with several countries via formal trade agreements and has often established trade clearing accounts between the central bank of the trading partner and the Bank of China. These agreements have provided for settlement of trade accounts in foreign exchange, gold, or specified commodities.

New Articles of Association, which make substantial changes in the BOC, were ratified by the State Council in September 1980 with immediate effect. They are set out in Appendix A. Aside from the already-mentioned transformation from a partly private enterprise into a totally state-owned bank, the number of bank directors was drastically reduced, the second-tier, State Council-appointed board of supervisors was formally established, powers were expanded (or at best made express), and bank capital was increased 150 percent to RMB 1 billion.

The document made expressly clear some points that had been obscure or uncertain.[6] The BOC may organize and participate in "international syndicated loans." RMB-denominated deposits by foreign account holders are to be subject to the approval of the People's Bank of China. Apparently the BOC may only take deposits and make loans in RMB if they are related to its foreign exchange business. The BOC was empowered to issue "foreign currency bonds and other negotiable securities" on behalf of the People's Republic under delegated authority. The bank's authority to invest in other banks or set up subsidiary companies is expressly made. Overseas branches and those in Hong Kong and Macao are now given open-ended authority to engage in any kind of banking operation, business, or transaction permitted by the laws prevailing in their respective locations. Domestic BOC branches are not given this flexibility.

The view expressed by most sources that the People's Bank of China exercises "day-to-day supervision" over the Bank of China is contested by some, including those within the Bank of China itself. While it is true that some members of the Bank of China's Board of Directors and Board of Supervisors are senior officials of the People's Bank, and that the BOC must look to the People's Bank each day for a supply of RMB to reimburse those selling foreign exchange to the BOC, the notion of "day-to-day" supervision is hard to comprehend. The Bank of China's new Articles of Association make no mention whatsoever of any reporting or supervision by the PBOC. The only supervision appears to be by the bank's own board of directors and board of supervisors as well as the State Council. The GAEC exercises control through setting and supervision of exchange controls and licensing allocations from the BOC accounts of state and collective enterprise.

Structure and Personnel

As stated above, the BOC is directly under the State Council and may be supervised by the PBOC.[7] Its headquarters are separate from the PBOC and overlook Tienanmen Square. BOC's honorary chairman is Oioo Peixin and its president is Bu-Ming. The president is the chief executive officer. In late 1981 Chang Yanging was variously reported to be honorary chairman, president, and acting chairman. The author has not discovered, at the time of writing, which position he holds.

The headquarters operations are led by the president, under whom serve six vice-presidents and nine general managers, with a general staff of about 500. The role of the board of supervisors is unclear. Its membership and its new tasks under the revised Articles of Association are obscure and appear to overlap those of the board of directors. In the past it has audited and signed the BOC's published balance sheets. It need meet only once a year. However, the two boards have been meeting more frequently—their sixth joint meeting was held in November 1981.

Operations are conducted through 77 domestic branches, as of July 1980 (consolidated from 90 open in early 1980), and five overseas branches and two representative offices, as of November 1981, some of which themselves direct subbranches. Preparations for additional overseas branches in Paris and Tokyo were well in hand by mid-1981 through the conversion of representative offices that were open since mid-1981.

The bank's head office is structured around nine departments, a framework that was modified slightly in late 1979 or early 1980. Not all these departments have counterparts, even in the largest branch offices.

International (Banking) Department: As the BOC maintains correspondent relations with almost one thousand banks and their thousands of branches, this department oversees the establishment, maintenance, and conduct of such relations. The department is primarily a formulator of policies and rules, with day-to-day bank contact going through domestic and overseas branches. Oversight is concentrated on ensuring proper collections by foreign banks acting for the BOC and interpreting letters of credit and agency duties under credit agreements with foreign government export-import banks, such as England's Export Credits Guarantee Department (ECGD) and France's Compagnie Francaise d'Assurance pour le Commerce Extérieur (COFACE). Visits both by and to foreign banks are arranged.

General Coordination Department: This department is in liaison with the GAEC and acts to "coordinate the foreign exchange earnings retained by provinces, municipalities, and enterprises."[8] It also makes recommendations to the GAEC on allocation of foreign exchange to local authorities.

Foreign Exchange (or Management of Funds) Department: This department is central planner, allocater, and executive decision maker on foreign exchange operations. It issues instructions for raising of funds in money markets (for example, Eurodollars in London or Asia dollars in Singapore), interbank money market operations, spot and future foreign exchange sales and purchases (generally through London or in the case of Hong Kong dollars via that branch), and transfers funds between the bank's accounts. The department balances the bank's accounts daily through two operations: first, receipt of "information on foreign exchange priorities and needs of provinces and municipalities from four other bank departments (international, credit, accounting, and banking) to which the regional authorities report"[9]; and second, execution of transfers between foreign banks with which the BOC has correspondent accounts.

Credit (Management) Department: This department participates in the negotiation of financing for central government projects and authorizes payment of foreign exchange portions of approved projects. Local project negotiations are handled by branch credit staff, but the headquarters' department must authorize the credit. The department processes documents, payments, and, where applicable, the application for foreign export-import bank funds under general credit agreements between the export-import bank involved and the BOC.

Accounting Department: The accounting and record-keeping functions are centralized within this department, which operates a computer system linked to the bank's computers in Hong Kong and London. The Hong Kong branch in turn shares its computer with the local "sister banks." The bank's balance sheets, including those filed with regulatory authorities in London and Hong Kong, are probably prepared by this department.

Banking Department: Operating at the center of day-to-day operations, all banking transactions go through, or are reported to, the banking department. One section deals with invisibles, including nontrade transactions, such as diplomatic salaries and expenses, shipping, insurance, communications (including post office accounts), remittances, and taxes.

International Financial Research Department: This group's work is divided on a regional basis. There are seven regional groupings; North and South America are joined together, but Europe, Eastern Europe, and the USSR are treated as separate regions. Special-function sections exist, and a general research office monitors and assesses worldwide economic trends and problems, including activities of international financial organizations. A library division and publication unit are maintained.

Personnel Department and Administrative Department: These departments are largely self-descriptive, but it should be noted that the latter proposes the bank's own budget.

This administrative structure is somewhat mirrored at branch level in major cities, with the branches having fewer departments. The detailed operation of one branch has been described elsewhere.[10] The Shanghai branch, the BOC's largest with a staff of over 400, has three business departments: banking, credit, and accounting. The banking department operates in four sections: Foreign Currency Deposit section, Overseas Chinese Service section, Letter of Credit section, and Collections section. The branch also has an Accounting Department. Domestic branches are concentrated along the coast (64 percent), and the largest concentration is in Guangdong Province (25 percent). Major branches, for example, often operate satellite offices or subbranches in tourist hotels and at airports.

The bank is experimenting with decentralization. Branches in other parts of the country are being granted broader discretionary powers by the head office. Direct lending to local enterprises and joint ventures, deposit taking from foreigners, and the issuing of guarantees are all being carried out by branches in Guangzhou, Shanghai, Fuzhou, and Tianjin. Broad limits, including maximum amounts, have been set, and, while the policy is experimental, it is in line with widespread efforts to decentralize economic implementation, if not planning. Foreign exchange planning is still highly centralized, and the establishment of the GAEC, as well as the 1980 exchange-control regulations, reaffirm that position.

The staff of the BOC is well trained, and Western bankers who deal with the BOC, including those inside China, are uniform in stating that the staff is intelligent and competent. However, the BOC's restricted role in recent decades has limited most of its domestic branch staff's exposure to simple import/export transactions. A certain lack of sophistication and confidence was noted in 1979 and 1980 when the BOC first started to approach unaccustomed transactions, such as commercial and syndicated loans.[11] Reluctance to conclude long-negotiated syndicated loans in 1979 may, in part, be explained by the bank staff's relative ignorance when first approaching modern Western banking terminology and the legal concepts involved, rather than any fundamental disagreement on terms proposed in draft agreements. China's reluctance to take up funds under concluded agreements in 1980 is, however, a matter of price and policy decision, rather than sophistication. The bank is currently seeking to modernize its staff training and raise their educational level. For example, young staff are being sent to in-house courses and schools run by London banks. These programs are for selected staff and last from 18 to 24 months.

Capitalization

All banks controlled by the People's Republic of China increased their capitalization in 1976. The BOC went from RMB 19.8 million to RMB 400 million. This may have been done simply to increase the ratio of capital to liabilities, but it also appears to have had a political purpose.[12] At the end of the 1978 financial year the BOC's capitalization was still RMB 400 million, or about U.S.$250 million at January 1980 exchange rates. In September 1980 capitalization was again boosted to RMB 1 billion, then approximately equivalent to U.S.$670 million. Simultaneously, sister banks in Hong Kong increased their capitalization.

Balance Sheets and Assets

Generally speaking, the Bank of China has been financially sound, although it was suggested to the author that the bank almost went bankrupt during the Gang of Four period. During the years 1974 and 1975, when China ran a relatively large deficit, the for-

TABLE 3

Bank of China Balance Sheet, Selected Years, 1970-80
(in thousands of renminbi)

	1970	1975	Percentage Change (five years)	1978	1979	1980	Percentage Change (five years)
Assets							
Cash	23,987	39,457	64	53,411	61,369	69,040	75
Due from banks	2,900,154	8,491,659	193	12,694,431	18,061,959	22,310,246	163
Bills discounted and remittances bought	759,522	1,687,353	122	2,939,834	3,678,679	4,451,202	164
Loans and overdrafts	1,540,576	4,896,245	216	7,155,456	10,897,407	21,326,226	336
Securities and investments	15,115	49,135	225	95,208	115,963	189,736	286
Land, buildings, furniture, equipment	45,665	94,532	107	237,453	329,109	371,565	293
Sundry accounts receivable, including under forward contracts	324,678	648,132	100	1,024,132	1,275,044	1,422,949	120
Collections receivable for customers	197,081	411,251	109	653,021	1,052,866	1,383,466	236
Customers liabilities under letters of credit and guarantees	1,241,553	9,221,569	643	12,671,021	17,462,114	22,508,385	144
Trust assets	188,354	588,581	212	295,235	310,675	323,724	(45)
Other assets	54,411	101,273	86	887,815	978,372	1,663,490	1543
Total assets	7,291,103	26,229,143	260	38,707,316	54,222,560	76,020,029	190

Liabilities							
Due to banks	2,417,329	7,148,117	195	7,034,829	10,948,303	16,580,570	132
Deposits	2,707,565	7,370,578	172	15,769,585	21,540,488	30,937,440	320
Remittances and drafts outstanding	38,289	85,694	124	171,019	286,970	460,012	468
Sundry accounts payable and accounts payable under forward contracts	247,754	523,451	111	793,327	998,798	1,110,664	112
Other liabilities	77,573	128,137	65	194,596	235,675	160,656	25
Collections for customers	197,081	411,251	102	653,021	1,052,866	1,383,466	236
Letters of credit and guarantee	1,241,553	9,221,569	613	12,671,321	17,462,111	22,508,385	144
Trust liabilities	188,354	588,581	302	295,235	310,675	323,724	(46)
Total liabilities	7,115,503	25,477,378	258	37,582,931	52,835,889	73,464,917	188
Net worth							
Capital	19,800	400,000	1,920	400,000	400,000	1,000,000	150
Surplus	64,482	107,238	66	250,332	308,773	383,805	260
Reserves	81,809	177,079	117	309,430	447,097	706,937	299
Net profit, current year	9,507	67,494	610	164,622	230,801	464,371	588
Total net worth	174,599	751,815	318	1,124,385	1,386,671	2,555,113	240

eign exchange gap was filled by deposits from other banks.[13] Although coy about disclosing its balance sheet, the bank, for many years, has operated in Hong Kong, Singapore, and London, where it is required by law to file its balance sheet with the local registry of companies. The figures available through these banking authorities give some indication of the growth of the bank's activities.

The major development in the bank's balance sheet is the enormous growth of assets. One study of the ten-year period from 1969 to 1978 showed a growth of 23 percent per year over that period. Its assets in 1978 equaled those of the First National Bank of Chicago and totaled RMB 76 billion at the close of 1980. Obviously, such figures are modest for a country the size of China,[14] but it must be noted that China is a relatively small trading nation.[15] During a recent five-year period the bank's assets grew 76 percent or, stated differently, at an annual compound rate of almost 11 percent. Within these balance sheets it is interesting to note the dramatic increase in the valuation of land, buildings, and furniture. The tripling in value for these items is probably not unusual given the property prices in Hong Kong, London, and Singapore and the fact that these properties were probably undervalued in the past.[16] Also worthy of note is that the "other" column has grown tenfold. It would appear to be about time that this now-very-large category be broken down further to disclose its contents.[17] The two largest items are now the amounts due from banks and customers' liabilities under letters of credit and guarantees. Liabilities have grown at a compound rate of 11 percent. Remittances and drafts outstanding have also grown remarkably. Deposits alone have increased 250 percent. It is also seen that net worth has quadrupled to RMB 1.1 billion or U.S.$733 million. Surpluses and reserves are up 175 percent and 106 percent, respectively. Net profits have almost tripled (up 297 percent).

These figures are based on balance sheets filed with Hong Kong authorities or supplied to the author by the bank and reproduced in Table 3. These simplified balance sheets satisfy local regulations but, nonetheless, conceal many of the vital figures under larger "grab-bag" categories. While this lessens their usefulness, the data does enable us to see the picture of a conservative, financially sound, and growing institution.

FOREIGN-BASED OPERATIONS

The Bank of China, which controlled 17 overseas branches from Beijing before 1949, now operates 5: Hong Kong, London, Singapore, Luxembourg, and New York. The other branches were located in Burma, India, Cambodia, Pakistan, Malaysia, Indonesia, Japan, Vietnam, and the United States. The history of these branches is examined below. It also controls a substantial number of private-state banks through its investments in banking operations in Hong Kong, Macao, and Singapore. Additionally, the BOC claims ownership and control of the branches and assets of the International Commercial Bank of China, the name given to the former Bank of China branches, which remain under Nationalist control from Taiwan. That bank's main branches are in New York, Tokyo, and Sydney.[18] The dispute is currently dormant, and the BOC is about to open its own branch in Tokyo, having just recently opened a branch in New York.

Foreign Branches

Hong Kong

The Hong Kong branch is the BOC's largest overseas office. It controls the activities of other banks in the region affiliated with it or incorporated in the People's Republic of China—the so-called sister banks—as well as supervises other PRC-owned or -controlled businesses operating there.[19] The Hong Kong branch also contributes the largest portion of the BOC's profits. The BOC and its 13 sister banks (including the one in Macao) offer the same services as other Hong Kong financial institutions. They operate much like other private banking institutions in Hong Kong, competing for deposits, lending and borrowing funds, and facilitating international trade.[20]

The Hong Kong branch has played a particularly unique role among the overseas operations of the Chinese government. It has been the Beijing government's listening post and contact point for trade and finance since 1949. The bank, along with its sister banks and other commercial networks throughout Hong Kong, has enabled China to keep in touch with Western business practices in fields as diverse as shipping, insurance, and banking. The Hong Kong branch of the BOC has also been used as a focal point to receive foreign visitors without the need for political and cultural penetration into the People's Republic. Operating in the British territory under basic English law has also given Chinese enterprises thorough familiarity with certain common-law doctrines in the area of commerce and finance.[21] Their financial success also contributes to optimism about maintenance of the status quo after 1997, when the treaty leasing the New Territories portion of the crown expires. The resultant contacts have provided sufficient bases for Western bankers to evaluate the BOC. In Hong Kong the bank is thought of as "savvy, highly aggressive," and able to "compete favorably with many of the world's large private banks."[22] The politically and financially sensitive position Chinese bankers are in has led some to comment that China's banks have done more than be financially successful. "The top bankers from Peking are diplomats in all but name which puts solidarity into their dealings."[23]

The branch operates as a full commercial bank carrying out international operations on behalf of the BOC, as well as commercial and banking services for the local business community. The Hong Kong banking market is characterized by tremendous competitiveness, including a wide variety of nonprice competition. The BOC and its sister banks have always been competitive and, as of late, have occasionally taken a lead. Among the activities handled by the BOC and advertised to the public are the following: stock market purchases, sales, and transfers on behalf of customers; collection of dividends; collection of principal and interest on overseas deposits; sale of overseas property; management of overseas inheritance; handling of compensation claims; and miscellaneous, including the sale of RMB-denominated traveler's checks and credit cards useable in five Chinese cities.

However, these activities, some of which started only recently, are only secondary. The BOC and its sister banks are mainly concerned with doing what is necessary to facilitate China's trade and foreign exchange needs. Thus, short-term loans to local merchants and industries have historically been to those who stock or use products from the mainland. Such activity provides a firm base and will continue irrespective of changes that may occur in current policies of long-term financing and vigorous expansion.

The bank has an interest in or controls 13 sister banks—12 in Hong Kong and 1 in the territory of Macao. In 1973 these banks (identified in Table 4) had a total of 78 branches and handled an estimated U.S.$1.2 billion in foreign exchange. By 1976 this had increased to 5 BOC branch offices and 120 sister bank branches.

TABLE 4

Chinese Sister Banks in Hong Kong and Macao, May 1980

Name of Bank	Number of Branches		Location of Head Office
Nanyang Commercial Bank (HK)	21	(plus two agencies and Godown [Land] Co. subsidiary)	Hong Kong
Po Sang Bank	4		Hong Kong
Bank of Communications	20		Beijing
Sin Hua Trust, Savings, and Commercial Bank (HK)	19	(plus four suboffices and finance company)	Hong Kong (?)
Kwangtung Provincial Bank	15		Guangzhou
Kincheng Banking Corporation	13	(plus one agency)	Shanghai
China and South Sea Bank	12	(plus trust company subsidiary)	Shanghai
Hua Chiao Commercial Bank (HK)	10		Hong Kong
National Commercial Bank	10		Shanghai
Chiyu Banking Corporation (HK)	7		Hong Kong
China State Bank	11		Shanghai
Yien Yieh Commercial Bank	12		Shanghai
Banco Nam Tung (in Macao)	14		Macao

Note: "HK" indicates incorporated in Hong Kong. All others are incorporated in China. The Kwangtung Provincial Bank also operates branches in Singapore. There are some variations in the English spellings of some bank names in the group.

Sources: U.S., Government Research Aid no. R77-13-37 (July 1977); Christopher Lewis, "China's Banks: The Communist Capitalists," Far Eastern Economic Review, April 1, 1974, pp. 17-18; Deidra D. Dreamer, "Recent Financial Developments in China," East Asian Executive Reports 1 (October 15, 1979): 2, 12-16; and Y. C. Jao, Banking and Currency in Hong Kong (London: Macmillan, 1974), pp. 39, 288; Peat Marwick, Mitchell, Banking in Hong Kong (Hong Kong: Peat Marwick, Mitchell, 1980), p. 20; and Hong Kong's 1980 Telephone Directory.

TABLE 5

Chinese Sister Banks in Hong Kong: Deposits and Profits, 1975-79
(in millions of Hong Kong dollars)

	1975	1976	1977	1978	1979	Average Annual Percentage Increase
Deposits*						
Sister banks	12.2	13.4	15.8	21.2	30.0	36.2
All Hong Kong banks	36.3	44.0	53.0	60.0	68.0	21.8
Sisters' share as percent of total	34	30	30	35	44	
Net profits*						
Sister banks	116	195	230	306	551	

*Deposits and profits of sister banks are based on worldwide operations but exclude those of their deposit-taking subsidiaries. Inner reserves are excluded. These data are not directly comparable to that of Hong Kong banks as a whole, which report Hong Kong deposits alone.

Source: Data supplied by the 12 sister banks to the Hang Seng Bank, Hong Kong, research department and reported in Banker 131 (May 1981): 145.

By May 1980 these had expanded to 10 BOC branches and 168 sister bank branches.

These sister banks are mostly incorporated in China. The four or five incorporated in Hong Kong are believed to have residents of the People's Republic appointed by the PBOC to act as private shareholders. Those incorporated in China as joint state-private enterprises have small equity holdings by state enterprises inside China.[24] Even prior to 1949 there were government banks along with the BOC, the Bank of Communications, and the Kwangtung Provincial Bank.[25] These three and the others incorporated in China operated in Hong Kong under Nationalist government control but were taken over and reorganized by the People's Republic government. Their head offices in China were reorganized in 1952 as joint state-private banks, but the external branches in Hong Kong were, for obvious reasons, left with separate identities. The sister banks operate in concert with the local BOC branch. Their joint futures were further cemented together with the installation of joint computerization housed in the BOC's Hong Kong head office. They increased their capitalization at the same time as the BOC in 1980. The tightly controlled group has had great success in holding a large share of the territory's banking business both in the share of deposits and in loans, the latter being reflected in higher net profits. This is demonstrated in Table 5, which shows the deposits of sister banks to have grown almost twice as fast as those of the Hong Kong banking system as a whole.

PRC-controlled banks aggressively seek depositors among Hong Kong's 5 million residents. In a two-year period (1974-76) these banks opened 23 additional branches. Although statistical data on the sister banks is incomplete (only the locally incorporated banks are obliged to regularly report their local balance sheets), no one doubts their significance as competitors. The Nanyang Commercial Bank, whose accounts are reported, qualifies as quite a large bank. The 12 Hong Kong sisters held just over one-third of all Hong Kong bank deposits in 1975, but by 1979 they had increased that share to 44 percent, while at the same time profits were increased by almost 500 percent (see Table 5). By 1976 the Communist-controlled banks were collectively second in size only to the Hong Kong-Shanghai Bank.

The BOC and its sister banks recently took several measures to maintain their competitiveness, including the establishment of a jointly owned finance company similar to the higher-interest-rate-paying operations of other leading Hong Kong banks. The BOC proposes to offer trust-department facilities in the near future. U.S.-dollar-denominated deposit accounts are available. Significantly, the bank is providing support facilities for those trading with the People's Republic of China. These measures are discussed further at the close of this chapter.

Apparently, a large percentage of savings accounts with sister banks and the Bank of China are denominated in RMB. Conceived as China's offshore counterpart to the Singapore Asia-dollar market, these accounts first became available in 1970. There are obviously some disadvantages to such accounts. The foremost is that RMB fluctuates against both the United States and Hong Kong dollars. Additionally, local Hong Kong dollar accounts are more readily convertible and accessible. However, the advantages are significant. RMB accounts are tax free because, being booked by Beijing and merely handled on behalf of the head office, they are free of the 15 percent Hong Kong withholding tax on interest. China's banks also promote the stability of RMB as protection against currency devaluation. Further, the interest rate offered on RMB has occasionally been better than that of other Hong Kong-dollar deposit accounts, though not always better than Eurodollar deposit rates. This is significant, because nominally the Exchange Banks Association, of which the BOC is a member, sets upper limits on interest rates for deposits in different groups of banks.[26] It is said that the BOC has not been in compliance with these rules, but no members have complained, being understandably reluctant to cause offense. The limits do not apply to the smaller sister banks.

Not much is known of China's banking operations in Macao. The link with the BOC is clear. Banco Nam Tung's new manager is concurrently deputy general manager of the BOC in Hong Kong and was previously a senior official in the London branch. Historically, this was an important outlet for gold sales by China. Such sales have continued and may well expand as China succeeds in boosting gold production. Banco Nam Tung is capitalized in local currency (25 million patacas equals approximately U.S.$5 million)—the only bank to do so. Macao's banking laws were to be drastically amended in 1981, including stricter regulations and steps to enhance Macao as an offshore banking center and interbank money market. Banco Nam Tung with its 14 branches should be well placed to take advantage of increased growth in Macao's financial status. In November 1981 it comanaged a HK$240 million syndicated credit for a local borrower.

London

The London Branch of the BOC dates from 1929, when it was an affiliate of a predecessor. The traditional importance of this branch for both Nationalist and Communist governments is largely a reflection of the unique status of London as the world's international banking center. However, the People's Republic has other reasons for granting London high standing in its activities. The United Kingdom was one of the earliest, and for some time almost the only one, of the Western powers to recognize the new government, which it did in January 1950. Additionally, China's options were limited. Although sterling steadily declined as a trade currency, while the dollar predominated, switching trade into dollars would have been very difficult; the Korean War had ultimately caused a U.S.-PRC trade embargo and a mutual freezing of assets.

Until recently, the branch's chief function was to receive external sterling from Hong Kong and countries like Australia, where sterling is used as a medium of trade payments. The London branch would convert some of this into other hard currencies or gold to be used for payment of China's trade bills. It also handled RMB sales for future delivery. Such sales are still limited to traders required in their contracts to pay in RMB.

In the early 1970s the bank also facilitated a form of borrowing undertaken by the government of China. Although the BOC has correspondent accounts with numerous Western banks, their deposits with each other are normally kept in balance. However, when China has needed to pay for imports with foreign currency not yet available, the BOC has utilized "supplier credits." Under these arrangements the supplier of goods to China arranged credit with his bank. That bank then placed a deposit with the BOC, normally in London, which used the deposited funds to pay for China's imports. In this manner the Bank of China has taken an active role in the London interbank market.

The London branch is China's primary center for dealings on world money markets. Today the branch in London plays an active role in arranging and negotiating credit for China and its state enterprises. It assists the BOC in its expanding roles in international finance as both lender and borrower, particularly in Eurodollar transactions. With a staff of about two hundred (doubled within the decade), it does business with over two hundred British and Western banks in London. Its loan and government credit business are described elsewhere in this book.

The branch collects deposits, particularly from local Chinese, for remittance to relatives inside China. To increase these deposits, as well as for other reasons, subbranches were opened in London and, in late 1979, in Manchester. Because several other banks with ethnic markets (for example, Indian and Pakistani) have found it profitable to open numerous branches in British cities where people from their homelands are clustered, it is quite conceivable that, as in Hong Kong, subbranches may proliferate elsewhere in the United Kingdom.

Singapore

As in Hong Kong, the BOC branch in Singapore acts in many ways as the unofficial embassy of the People's Republic. It is taken as the voice of China and has in very recent years been treated as a government entity by Singapore authorities. The bank operates through a main branch with at least three subbranches and has effective control of Kwangtung Provincial Bank. The latter is incorporated in China with several branches in Hong Kong as well as Singapore. Kwangtung Provincial and the BOC are the only Chinese banks with foreign branches other than those in Hong Kong. The BOC is also said to control some local trading companies.

Singapore is increasingly important as a trade partner with China. Some joint venture deals between Chinese and Singapore companies have been announced. As early as 1970 Chinese exports to Singapore totaled U.S.$100 million. The BOC has also facilitated the RMB requirements of Singapore-based traders.[27] This factor, combined with the proximity of Malaysia and Indonesia, both countries with substantial overseas Chinese populations, has reportedly caused the BOC to repeatedly press Malaysian authorities for permission to reestablish a branch in Malaysia. This was done without success in 1970.[28] BOC staff denied this report in an interview with the author.

The Singapore branch has suffered somewhat because of political difficulties between the governments of Singapore and China. For some time the Malaysian government and the Republic of Singapore government have recognized neither Taiwan nor Beijing as the government of China. Therefore, no manager or representative from China was allowed to visit Singapore from 1949 until 1979, even though the bank was permitted to operate. These political difficulties included a major row over the bank's alleged lack of liquidity. The BOC's clashes with Malaysian, and subsequently with Singapore, authorities merit being set out at length because of the serious nature of the allegations made against the BOC and the ensuing consequences.

Shortly after becoming an independent nation, the Federation of Malaya (later Malaysia) amended its Bank Act in 1958 to prohibit foreign banks over one-half owned by a foreign government from dodoing business within Malaya. This led to the cessation of business by the BOC's Kuala Lumpur and Penang branches on April 1, 1959. The BOC's Singapore branch was not immediately affected, because Singapore did not join the federation until September 1963. Sometime in February 1965,[29] when Singapore was contemplating secession from the Malaysian Federation, the government of Malaysia informed the BOC that it must close its Singapore operation within six months.[30] The BOC's reactions included informing the government that closure would make it impossible for the BOC "to meet its obligations."[31] As a result Bank Negara Malaysia agreed to lend the BOC S$12 million in July 1965. The loan, at 6.5 percent interest, was secured by a floating charge on all of the BOC's local assets and a legal second mortgage on certain properties. Interestingly, the BOC had already mortgaged these properties to the Overseas Chinese Banking Corporation and was therefore already a borrower—this at the height of the Cultural Revolution, when official Chinese publications boasted that China was a country free of all foreign debt.[32] The situation must have involved great political pressures, as Singapore was a mere month away from breaking with the federation. Significantly, six months after the BOC was served notice of closure, Bank Negara took over direct day-to-day control of the BOC from August 5 until August 17, 1965, a period that included Singapore's independence from Malaysia on August 9. What happened during the next two years is particularly obscure, but it seems likely that the BOC defaulted on the loan, or refused to continue repaying Bank Negara for political reasons.

In July 1968 that bank, in pursuit of its claim for S$7 million, obtained a Singapore High Court order freezing the BOC's assets and served garnishment orders on 34 other Singapore banks. All of the amount was recovered through a sheriff's garnishment on the BOC's account with the Chartered Bank (later to become the Standard Chartered Bank). The Chartered Bank paid over that sum. Presumably, the BOC felt it had done so wrongly, because the Chinese press described this proceeding as one in which "the reactionary Singapore authorities . . . brazenly worked hand in glove with British Chartered Bank in robbing the Singapore branch," an "act of piracy"; and in September 1968 the "Chartered Bank was compelled to admit that its holding up the deposits was invalid and paid back S$1.5 million."[33] The sum of S$1.5 million referred to is in reality more likely to be merely the balance left in the BOC's account after the garnishment, which was paid over to the BOC when its account was unfrozen by the court. No Singapore source even hints that the Chartered Bank was asked to pay back, or paid back, any of the sum garnished.

Freezing the BOC's assets had, in the words of the commissioner for banking, threatened to grind the city's business life to a halt. A subsequent investigation and partial audit revealed that the BOC was in violation of minimum liquid reserve ratios for 128 days from July 1968 through March 1969. In particular, it was charged that the BOC continued to carry as an asset the sum garnished against its Chartered Bank account, and that in February 1969 the deficit in minimum reserves reached almost S$8 million on total liabilities to depositors of S$57.7 million.

Fearful of a run on the bank and because the BOC refused all subsequent inspections and demands to show records and file reports, the commissioner prosecuted and successfully sought the maximum fine of S$1,000 per day for the 128-day shortages. The BOC refused the summons, did not appear, and refused receipt of the May 1969 judgment. Its only response was to hold political rallies outside the bank for several days. A few days thereafter the Ministry of Finance responded to the rallies, massive withdrawals, and offenses by threatening cancellation of the BOC's license and withdrawing clearinghouse facilities for all BOC checks as of May 22, 1969. The ministry's statement illustrates the bad feelings between the parties.

> The Singapore branch of the Bank of China is clearly claiming for itself extraterritorial rights which foreign businesses enjoyed before World War II in certain Treaty Ports in China. These extraterritorial rights were imposed by foreign imperialists upon China as a result of unequal treaties. These enabled foreigners to be exempt from the laws of China. That the Bank of China regards itself as exempt from the laws is demonstrated by recent actions.

The statement then listed five offenses of the Penal Code of the Banking Ordinance.

> In the light of these repeated violations of the laws . . . the Ministry of Finance is reviewing the conditions [of the BOC's continued permission to operate]. . . . The long-term future of the bank depends on whether it will obey the laws of the Republic or whether it will persist in the absurd notion that it enjoys extraterritorial rights.

Earlier in May 1969 the BOC had taken weak retaliation by refusing all letters of credit for imports from China that were not issued by it and expressly stating that the Chartered Bank's letters of credit would not be accepted. The BOC continued banking for 19 months without local clearing facilities. The reasons for the resumption of clearinghouse operations or the government's terms for settlement were not disclosed, but presumably China found it possible to give some assurances in late 1970 that were not possible earlier.

What is to be made of these extraordinary incidents? Several comments are in order. The events are a strong reminder that the BOC has played a political, as well as economic, role. Present emphasis on pragmatism cannot easily change the fact of life that the BOC is an instrument of government policy and that in places where it represents the main or only permanent voice of China (for example, Hong Kong and, until 1980, Singapore), it is a political instrument. However, the particular actions from 1965 to 1968, and the BOC's shocking behavior of 1969, must be attributed to three factors: China's internal turmoil during the Cultural Revolution, its external battle with Malaysia over charges of illicit support of guerrillas, and its dispute with Singapore over nonrecognition of the People's Republic.[34]

There is a danger of making too much of these events. The BOC's actions were like the bursting of a boil that had festered for a long time between Malaysia/Singapore and China. Like a burning fever the Cultural Revolution angered the wound and brought it to a head. The international banking community had not seen actions like these for some time and can only hope that they shall not be repeated for at least several more decades. Certainly, the events are from a different era in Chinese domestic and foreign affairs, an era unlikely to be soon repeated. Recent relations between Singapore and China are markedly improved. The author was told by BOC officials in Guangzhou that the new Singapore policy toward China permitted the appointment of a new manager from Beijing.[35] Relations between Standard Chartered Bank and the BOC are also excellent. The incident, like many problems, is today blamed by the BOC staff on the disruption caused by the Gang of Four.

Luxembourg

A new branch of the BOC opened in Luxembourg in early 1979. It was specifically designed to facilitate China-European Economic Community trade and was the first branch expansion by the BOC into a new country since 1949. The branch is staffed by personnel who have been trained at certain merchant banks on the Continent and in London.

Tokyo, Paris, and New York

The BOC's application for a New York branch was approved in time for a late 1981 opening. The BOC's former U.S. representative Zhang Xueyao is the new branch manager. The Tokyo representative office may also become a branch. A representative office opened in Paris in June 1981 but without an immediate indication of when, or if, a branch is planned.

Other Claimed Foreign Bank Branches

It was mentioned above that the BOC was under the control of the Nationalist government during the Revolution. At that time the BOC had 21 overseas branches. When the Chinese mainland fell to the Communists, the management in each overseas branch had to choose whether to follow Chairman Mao or Generalissimo Chiang. Branches in London, Hong Kong, and Singapore chose to come under Communist control. They were joined by branches in Burma, Cambodia, India, Indonesia, Malaysia, and Pakistan. All of the latter have subsequently been closed voluntarily or donated to the host government in order to avoid nationalization (as in the case of Pakistan) or confiscated because of war or hostilities (for example, Bombay and Calcutta).[36] Differences between the Malaysian government and the People's Republic of China required the closing of the Kuala Lumpur and Penang offices in 1959.

Branches in New York, Tokyo, Saigon, Sydney, Osaka, Cholon, and Bangkok all opted for Nationalist control. On December 15, 1971, the government of Taiwan changed the name of the bank to the International Commercial Bank of China (ICBOC) and increased its capital from U.S. $500,000 to U.S. $25 million. These moves were designed to counter the effects of increasing diplomatic recognition of the government of the People's Republic of China. It was felt that the ICBOC's legal status would be more secure in Western countries if the role of private investment was strengthened. Beijing's response was to reinstate its old claim to all of the old Bank of China and Bank of Communications assets.

> All of the assets of the branches of these two banks in the provinces and in foreign countries along with the head offices of the two banks and only the People's Bank of China and the head offices of the two banks have the right to dispose of them. It is absolutely impermissible for anyone by any means to appropriate or sell them illegally.[37]

The possibility of political or legal disputes erupting over these claims cannot be entirely discounted. It has been almost 11 years since China last stated a claim on the ICBOC's assets. Present silence on this dispute, like all of those with Taiwan, cannot be assumed to represent any change in basic policies. The dispute has merely been submerged for the moment, not resolved. Nonetheless, the present leadership's overall pragmatic policy indicates that, as with offshore oil claims against Taiwan, China will bide its time. It will be slow to launch an attack that would put at risk the cooperation of Western and Asian nations and enterprises in supplying it with technology and finance. The author was unable to discover if the issue arose in steps to open the BOC's New York branch in November 1981. If it was not confronted it may give rise to the implication that the International Commercial Bank of China's New York branch has de facto been accepted as separate.

EXPANDING ROLES FOR THE BOC

Present policy is for the BOC to continue its overseas activities and expansion abroad. In a 1979 address to Western and Chinese bankers in Hong Kong, Managing Director Lin Jixin stated that the BOC will increase the number of foreign banks with which it has business relations (already almost 1,000), open branches in Tokyo and New York and a representative office in Paris (branches in Frankfurt, Germany, and Switzerland have also been mentioned by bank officials), and participate in Eurocurrency and other types of syndicated lending.[38] Most of those goals have been realized.

To further that policy the BOC has given some of its key branches, both in China and outside, more authority and discretion to deal directly with local Chinese enterprises and foreign companies. This is particularly true in the case of joint venture arrangements, and the policy apparently extends to the sister banks, which were encouraged during 1979 to adopt "capitalist methods" as long as they are profitable. The only self-imposed limitation is on speculation, as these commercial banks will not invest for their own accounts in Hong Kong's wild stock markets.[39]

The most recent surge in the expanding role of the bank can be said to have started in late 1978. At that time the bank started to develop new techniques and new relationships. Contacts increased through visits from Western banks, and BOC delegations traveled to the United Kingdom, Belgium, West Germany, and Switzerland. Led by Bu-Ming, president of the BOC, the delegation met with the chairmen of all major British clearing banks and merchant banks. It was here that China first hinted of its willingness to openly borrow medium- and long-term credit.[40]

China has already started to use its banks for investment in various Hong Kong property transactions. The Kincheng and China State banks have invested about HK$200 million in prime business property. The Xinhua News Agency paid HK$72 million for the erection of a 23-story hotel-office building. Both the Bank of China and Nanyang Commercial Bank provided 100 percent financial guarantees for the operations of the two Communist-controlled Hong Kong investment companies—Kiu Kowong Investment Corporation and Sun Company.

The Bank of China was reportedly involved in another property transaction for £100 million in the New Territories of Hong Kong in the township of Luk Yeung Sun Chuen.[41] The BOC was also involved in financing for the Hong Kong mass transit system.

With these transactions and those of other controlled companies, China has joined the Hong Kong property boom. The BOC's involvement in the property market caused much comment and was often referred to as "commercialized Communism."[42] That Communist-controlled banks should profit from free-enterprise capitalism struck many as highly ironic. Others speculated on the significance of property loans and purchases of land that China already claims to own. After all, the People's Republic has never accepted any of the leases of Hong Kong and the New Territories to the United Kingdom. Some speculated that China would not pay for land it already owned if it had any intention of raising the lease issue or occupying the New Territories upon that particular lease's expiration.

Whatever the political implications, China's real estate actions make economic sense in a city where fortunes are made every day in property. Given China's need for foreign exchange, entry into real estate was logical. Outside its borders, China has always pursued its objectives pragmatically, even when called upon to participate in land speculation.

The BOC and its sister banks launched full-fledged finance companies. Those already established include the BOC's China Development Finance Company, capitalized at U.S. $9.7 million and set up in April 1979 to market certificates of deposit, stocks, securities, and gold. This new company is partially owned by three Chinese-controlled insurance companies. Another company was set up in April 1979 by Sin Hua Trust, Savings, and Commercial Bank.

As a result of its expanding relations with foreign banks, the Nanyang Commercial Bank placed interbank deposits for the first time with a U.S. bank, the Bank of America, in the amount of RMB 5 million.

Syndicated Loans and Bond Issues

A development that caused much excitement in the international banking community was the Hong Kong branch's participation in a U.S. $42 million syndicated loan to Gloxin, a subsidiary of the Hong Kong-based Sun Hung Kai, a company with close ties to the People's Republic of China. This syndicated loan was arranged by Paribas Asia to fund building of a U.S. $55 million downtown office tower. The terms called for a period of four to seven years at an interest rate of 1 percent over the London interbank offered rate (LIBOR). Loan negotiations were completed within three months, and the loan was finalized on June 6, 1979. Participants included the Bank of America, the Bank of Montreal, the Bank of Tokyo, Dresdner Bank, and Kleinwort Benson (HK), each participating for an amount equal to that of the BOC. A larger portion of the loan was taken by Banque de Paris et des Pays-Bas, of which Paribas Asia is a subsidiary. The Bank of Tokyo came in at the last minute, when it learned that the BOC was participating.[43]

Only four months later the BOC took another major step by becoming one of three colead managers in a HK$55.7 million, ten-year synidcated loan. The other managers were Chase Manhattan of New York and Hong Kong-Shanghai Banking Corporation, with Chase acting as the agent bank. This was the first time that the BOC took part in lead management of such a loan, and it was its first syndicated lending in Hong Kong dollars. The borrower was China Cement Company (H.K.), which is 20 percent owned by Kiu Yie, a Beijing-controlled company. China Cement's chairman is Li Ka-shing, a Hong Kong businessman, who was recently named to the board of the China International Trust and Investment Corporation.[44]

The Bank of China also participated in a U.S. $150 million syndicated loan for the African Development Bank put together by a group of banks led by Chase Manhattan. The 12-year loan was funded by a group of 37 banks.[45] Acting on its own, the BOC arranged a loan totaling HK$18 million (U.S. $3.7 million) to a newly formed Hong Kong company involved in the construction of a luxury residential complex in Guangdong Province. The loan is at an interest rate

TABLE 6

Bank of China Participation in International Bank Transaction Publicized in 1978–May 1981
(in millions of U.S. dollars unless otherwise indicated)

Date	Type of Participation	Form of Credit	Amount	Purpose
Early 1978	Lender and guarantor	Loan	£100	Property development in New Territories
Early 1978	n. a.	Revolving credit	n. a.	Hong Kong Mass Transit System
April 1979	Joint venture participant	Capitalization	$9.7	Finance company
June 1979	Co-lender	Syndicated loan	$42	To Gloxin for office
October 1979	Colead man-ager	Syndicated loan	$55.7	To China Cement Company for expansion
October 1979	Co-lender	Syndicated loan	$150	African Development Bank
December 1979	Colead man-ager	Eurobond issue	$30	With Midland Bank for Crédit Lyonnaise
January 1980	Lender	Single-bank loan	$3.7	To undisclosed Hong Kong property company

January 1980	Colead manager	Eurobond issue	$25	For Long-Term Credit Bank of Japan
April 1980	Joint venture partner	Capitalization	$2	Establishment of CICC Finance Limited, a merchant bank
April 1980	Joint venture partner	Capitalization	$1	Merchant bank partnership with Kincheng Bank and Bank of Tokyo
June 1980	Agent bank	Loan	$42	CICC Finance Limited loan for construction of hotel in China
March 1981	Co-lender	Syndicated loan	$72	To Great Wall Hotel, Joint Venture of Beijing loan by Nordic Bank
May 1981	Comanager	Syndicated loan	$50	To Finmeccanica, S.p.a.
May 1981	Comanager	Syndicated loan	S$100	To Parkway Properties, Limited

n.a. = not applicable

<u>Sources</u>: Contemporary news accounts cited within notes to Chapter 3.

of 10 percent for a two-year period; it is believed to be the first Chinese loan to a Hong Kong company engaged in compensation trade in China.[46] The BOC's main publicized lending is summarized in Table 6.

Joint Venture Merchant Banking

In early 1980 the Hong Kong branch of the BOC announced that it was establishing a joint venture merchant bank. Presumably this would be incorporated in Hong Kong. The BOC's partner was the First National Bank of Chicago, which had initiated the proposal. First National was to have a 30 percent interest and named one of its merchant bankers as the first managing director. Other participants were the Industrial Bank of Japan (30 percent) and China Resources Company (10 percent), a Beijing-controlled trading company situated in Hong Kong and second only to the BOC as China's source of foreign exchange income in Hong Kong. The bank, called the CICC Finance Limited, will have a paid-up capital equivalent to U. S. $2 million and an authorized capital of U. S. $5 million.[47] The announced aim was to promote trade and investment in the Pacific Basin and among the shareholders' countries. Obviously, the bank was also designed to give the BOC expertise in another area of international finance. In June 1980 the CICC participated in a U. S. $42 million syndicated loan to help finance construction of a hotel in China.

A few days later the BOC announced it would participate in another joint venture with its sister bank, Kincheng Banking Corporation, and the Bank of Tokyo. The Kincheng-Tokyo Finance Company will be incorporated in Hong Kong and have an authorized capital equivalent to U. S. $1 million. Its main objectives will be to provide trade financing and guarantees, as well as to assist joint venture businesses with China.

SUMMARY

The BOC has demonstrated a generally modern, open, and innovative approach to international banking. Its creation of new merchant banking subsidiaries; participation as lender and manager of syndicated credits; entry into new consumer and commercial activities in Hong Kong and London; opening of new overseas branches and offices; upgrading of staff; cooperating with Chase Manhattan, Kuhn Loeb, and more recently, Merrill Lynch; and expanding correspondent banking—taken together, these represent a historic blossoming into a significant force in international banking. The growth of overseas offices is in contrast with the shutdowns and reductions that took place from 1949 to 1965. The acceptance of the bank in the community has softened the memory of its unhappy clashes with Malaysian, Singapore, and British banks and authorities.

This growth has been combined with a great increase in profits and even growth in relevant portions of its balance sheet. The stature of the bank within China has risen correspondingly. While the PBOC is attempting to reassert its authority, and the BOC's relationship to the GAEC is still being worked out, the BOC's role in economic planning and oversight has clearly increased.

NOTES

1. Leo Goodstadt, "Peking Elevates the Bank of China's Status," Euromoney 11 (September 1979): 70.

2. Ibid.

3. David L. Denny, "International Finance in the People's Republic of China," in China: A Reassessment of the Economy, U.S., Congress, Joint Economic Committee (Washington, D.C.: Government Printing Office, 1975), p. 659.

4. See details in Chapter 1 under subheading "Exchange Rate Policy."

5. The interrelationship between various state agencies involved in international trade is seen in Christopher Howe, China's Economy—A Basic Guide (London: Elek Books, 1978).

6. Pauline Loong, "Bankers, Set Your Hearts at Ease," Far Eastern Economic Review, January 9, 1981, p. 53.

7. Material on the structure of BOC headquarters and the Shanghai branch is largely based on Nicholas Ludlow and James Stepanek, "Inside the Bank of China," China Business Review 7 (July-August 1980): 9-13, which in turn is based on material supplied to the National Council on U.S.-China Trade by the BOC. The author has also relied upon his own interviews with BOC officials and a published address by a bank staff member, Chang Yen-nian, "Financing Possibilities," in China's New Economic Strategies (Switzerland: Zentrung für Unternehmungsfuhrung [Economic Management Center], 1980), p. 124.

8. Ludlow and Stepanek, "Inside," p. 9.

9. Ibid., p. 10.

10. Ibid.

11. Barry Kramer, "Borrowing from Capitalism," Wall Street Journal, May 8, 1979, p. 40, col. 1.

12. "Bank of China: Still a Touch of Glamour," Financial Times, June 10, 1977, p. 29, col. 5; and Dick Wilson, "How Banks Work in China," Banker 130 (January 1980): 24.

13. "Bank of China," Financial Times, June 10, 1977, p. 29.

14. James Stepanek, "A Ten-Year Profile of the Bank of China," China Business Review 6 (September-October, 1979): 41.

15. See Chapter 1 for background information on China's trade.

16. Wilson, "How Banks Work," p. 20.

17. Ibid.

18. Christopher Lewis, "China's Banks: The Communist Capitalists," Far Eastern Economic Review, April 1, 1974, pp. 17-18.

19. Edward Lupton, "Hong Kong's Role in Sino-Western Trade," in China's Trade with the West, ed. Arthur Stahnke (New York: Praeger, 1972), p. 201. These nonbanking operations include 50 department stores, 2 insurance companies, shoe store chains, several publishing houses, and numerous restaurants. Also see Melinda Liu, "Hong Kong Banking: China Makes Its Presence Felt," Financial Times, July 19, 1978, p. 28, col. 1.

20. Y. C. Jao, Banking and Currency in Hong Kong (London: Macmillan, 1974), documents the roles of these banks in the context of all major financial institutions in Hong Kong. More generally, see Liu, "Hong Kong Banking," p. 28; Lewis, "China's Banks," p. 17; Lupton, "Hong Kong's Role, p. 202; and Barry Kramer, "People's Banker," Wall Street Journal, December 1, 1976, p. 1.

21. Gene T. Hsiao, The Foreign Trade of China: Policy, Law, and Practice (Berkeley and Los Angeles: University of California Press, 1977). According to Hughes, "The colony is China's most useful point of contact with the foreign devils outside the Middle Kingdom . . . [where] a faceless miscellany of party cadres . . . can use Hong Kong as a listening-post." See Richard Hughes, Borrowed Place, Borrowed Time, 2d ed. (Hong Kong: André Deutsch, 1976), p. 42. Chinese enterprises have been involved in litigation in the colony. See Alan Smith, "Trade with Hong Kong," in Law and Politics in China's Foreign Trade, ed. Victor Li (Seattle: University of Washington Press, 1977), pp. 189-219.

22. Kramer, "People's Banker," p. 1, col. 1.

23. Lewis, "China's Banks," p. 18.

24. Deidra Dreamer, "Recent Financial Developments in China," East Asian Executive Reports 1 (October 15, 1979): 12-16.

25. Jao, "Banking," p. 39.

26. Kramer, "People's Banker," p. 1; also described in Jao, "Banking," pp. 54-56.

27. William Triplett, "The Banking Industry," in Doing Business with China: American Trade Opportunities in the 1970s, ed. William Whitson (New York: Praeger, 1974), p. 197.

28. Lawrence Fairhill, "A Peek into Peking's Banks," Finance 89 (October 7, 1971): 30.

29. There is a wide variation in the general accounts referring to these Singapore-BOC disputes. I have tried to rely on contemporaneous accounts in the local Singapore press and Beijing Review. The local articles that I examined appeared virtually every day in Straits Times, from May 8, 1969 (p. 11) through May 22, 1969 (p. 1) and on December 18 and December 23, 1970. Sources with different dates or sequences of events include S. Jayakumar, "The Singapore Branch of the Bank of China and Exercise of 'Extra-territorial

Rights,'" American Journal of International Law 64 (1970): 371-74 (the most complete summary); Fairhall, "A Peek," p. 30; Dick Wilson, "Bank of China in Singapore," Banker, vol. 122 (February 1972); idem, "The Bank of China Steps Out," Banker 124 (February 1974): 105-10; Newsweek, May 26, 1969, p. 103; and Triplett, "The Banking Industry," pp. 190-209. I could not discover why Malaysia did not immediately apply its 1958 act to BOC Singapore as soon as the city joined the federation in 1963.

30. "Current Developments," China Quarterly, no. 24 (1965), pp. 211-12.

31. Straits Times, May 15, 1969.

32. Peking Review, May 30, 1969.

33. Ibid.

34. China's attitudes toward Singapore's authorities in 1969 are reflected in the following remarks from Peking Review, May 30, 1969, pp. 27, 29. "To suit the needs of their internal and external policies, the reactionary Singapore authorities have always been exerting their efforts to discriminate against [the BOC] and try to undermine its reputation and business . . . intimidate its responsible members . . . unreasonably demanding to check the bank's books." BOC staff "strongly rejected these preposterous demands."

35. Confirmed in Wilson, "How Banks Work," p. 25.

36. Tadao Miyashita, The Currency and Financial System of Mainland China, trans. T. R. McEwan (Seattle: University of Washington Press, 1966), p. 126; and Katharine Huang Hsiao, Money and Monetary Policy in Communist China (New York: Columbia University Press, 1971), p. 24.

37. Announcement by the People's Bank of China on March 13, 1970, quoted in Wilson, "The Bank Steps Out," p. 110.

38. "Trade with China," Economist," November 10, 1979, p. 106.

39. Wall Street Journal, August 2, 1978, p. 8, col. 2.

40. Times (London), August 17, 1978, p. 15, col. 4.

41. Melinda Liu, "Hong Kong Banking," p. 28, col. 1; and "China and Hong Kong in Joint Property Deal," Financial Times, August 31, 1978, p. 1, col. 6.

42. Hughes, Borrowed Place, Borrowed Time, p. 40, attributes the phrase to Chang Kuo-sin, who states further, "Outside China, Peking assumes the posture and reality of a hard-boiled and seasoned capitalist."

43. Melinda Liu, "Rock Bottom Terms Are a Must for Foreigners," Far Eastern Economic Review, September 21, 1979, pp. 61-63;

Wall Street Journal, June 7, 1979, p. 29, col. 6; and for further background, see Wall Street Journal, May 8, 1979, p. 40, col. 1.

44. Asian Wall Street Journal Weekly, October 29, 1979, p. 9, col. 4.

45. Ibid., October 18, 1979, p. 8.

46. Ibid., February 11, 1980, p. 8, col. 2.

47. Wall Street Journal, April 25, 1980, p. 18, col. 1.

3

THE ROLE OF FOREIGN BANKS

THE HISTORIC ROLE

In Chinese history foreign banks are equated with "foreign imperialism." The Communist party has blamed the role that foreign banks played in China for many of the ills of prerevolutionary Chinese society. In Chinese writings, foreign banks have continually been associated with foreign exploitation,[1] and undoubtedly foreign banks did play a major role in the Western domination of Chinese society in the 1800s and early 1900s.[2]

The primary function of foreign banks during those times was to provide short-term financing for the foreign trade of both foreign and Chinese merchants. They possessed an effective monopoly in international financing and, thus, constituted the foreign exchange market as well. Merchant banking activities carried out included industrial finance and long-term credit. Much of the long-term credit went to the government or its agencies.[3] Other functions included the issuing of currency (in the form of their own bank notes), handling remittances of overseas Chinese, and accepting local deposits (including those of wealthy Chinese). European banks, especially British ones, predominated. The short history of U.S. banking in prerevolutionary China largely involved short-term trade financing. U.S. banks, operating through branches or specialized banks, also carried out foreign exchange operations and offered limited consumer-banking services for U.S. citizens and companies, as did British banks for their counterparts. The U.S. banks, such as the American Express International Banking Corporation, Chase, and Cathay Trust,[4] had limited branch facilities and did not undertake major investments. In general, they were dwarfed by European banking operations and, later, by modern Chinese-owned banks.[5]

Postrevolutionary China

During the disturbances of the Revolution and immediately thereafter, many foreign banks voluntarily closed down and left. Some banks left merely because banking in China was no longer profitable during or immediately after the Revolution. Wage rises were forced, taxes increased, and inflation was rampant. To this were added labor problems brought on by anticapitalist Chinese staff. Some of the small handful of foreign banks that remained had their property expropriated. This was the case with U.S. banks, such as Chase, American Express, and First City National Bank, whose accounts were frozen during the Korean War. Other banks remained in China, and for various reasons, have continued to carry on banking activities to this day, albeit limited. There are two leading Western banks operating through branches in Shanghai: the Hong Kong-Shanghai Banking Corporation and the Chartered Bank. Reportedly, these two "British" banks* were allowed to remain in their limited capacity, the result of a deal between the United Kingdom and China whereby the Bank of China (BOC) was permitted to maintain its London branch.[6]

The Chartered Bank is part of the British banking group called Standard Chartered Bank. It has had a branch in Shanghai without interruption for 121 years. Traditionally, it has been managed by an expatriate British citizen. Since the Revolution its general staff is entirely local Chinese, most of whom are drawn from the local branch of the Bank of China. As of early 1980 Standard Chartered's work is almost entirely limited to the handling and negotiating of

---

*As this book goes to press the "British" status of the Hong Kong-Shanghai Banking Corporation is being called into question during its attempt to take over the Royal Bank of Scotland.

documentary credits, including advising other banks' credits to the BOC in Beijing and Shanghai. The bank handles credits from other banks, including those originating in the BOC. It handles a small amount of remittances from overseas Chinese.

Prior to the Revolution, Chartered Bank had 21 branches spread throughout China. After the Revolution, business conditions and regulations changed so much that these full-service branches were unprofitable. A settlement was negotiated with China in 1955-56 whereby all assets and buildings were closed and handed over to the Chinese. The Chartered Bank then took up its present rented premises in Shanghai. Its old building, prominent on the Bund, Shanghai's main commercial street, is now used for other purposes.

The Chinese have always required that the Chartered Bank have at least one Westerner from the home office inside China at all times. This meant that if the Shanghai representative went on holiday or home leave, another representative had to come, say from Hong Kong, to replace him during his absence. During late 1979 the Chinese agreed for the very first time to allow the representative, Peter Butler, to leave on a short holiday without a replacement being sent ahead.

The Chartered Bank hopes to be permitted to expand its activities within China. Indeed, the bank was allowed to accept foreign-currency deposits in late 1980. Bank officials view expansion as a distinct possibility but expressed some doubts whether or not it would be immediately profitable; but Chartered takes a long-term view in planning its China activities and might, therefore, expand operations, despite realizing that profits might not be easily obtainable in the short term. Expansion, if and when it comes, will be to large trade centers like Guangzhou. Chartered Bank acknowledges its relatively privileged position within China and attributes this to the historical fact that the bank was originally started to function primarily in China and India.

The Chartered Bank is subject to the foreign exchange rules of China and, therefore must, like all individuals and institutions, surrender its foreign exchange to the BOC within six days (under pre-1981 regulations). Receipts are surrendered within six days for bills from Hong Kong and 12 days for the rest of the world. These time periods seem to be based on mailing times. The Chartered Bank must pay Chinese taxes calculated on gross profits as well as a municipal tax on turnover. It was taxed at the 70 percent rate during 1979/80.

The colorful history of Standard Chartered's Asian operations includes a modern incident in China in 1969, during which time the

Shanghai branch manager, through no fault of his own, was imprisoned.[7] This incident requires an understanding of the uncontrolled turmoil in China during the Cultural Revolution. Red Guards (militant youth at the forefront of the Cultural Revolution's rampage) dragged the Chartered Bank's manager (who was just about to retire) and his wife from their home at 3:00 A.M. The manager was put in confinement, and his whereabouts were unknown for six months. His wife left the country before his release, and his total imprisonment lasted for two and one-half years. He has now peacefully retired, and his replacements have enjoyed tranquil relations since the end of the Cultural Revolution.

The Hong Kong-Shanghai Banking Corporation does business in its Shanghai branch under the name Hong Kong British Bank. Like Standard Chartered, the Hong Kong British Bank is staffed with local Chinese but managed by an expatriate sent by the Hong Kong headquarters. It is among the earliest and most important foreign banks in China, having fourteen branches there prior to the Revolution, three in 1952, and only one today. Aside from any "deal" with the United Kingdom, its continued presence in China may in part be attributed to the fact that it was founded in 1865 by a group of English merchants residing in China. It was the first "foreign" bank not controlled from abroad. The bank also had early official links, being one of three banks appointed to receive Chinese custom revenues after the revolution of 1911.[8]

The other two banks operating in China are the Overseas Chinese Banking Corporation and the Bank of East Asia. Unlike the two already discussed, both of these banks are not run by expatriates but by local people appointed by the head office of the parent bank. The Overseas Chinese Banking Corporation, registered in Singapore, is the parent bank of a group that in 1976 represented 22 percent of aggregate bank assets in Singapore. It has six overseas branches, two of which are in China—at Amoy and Shanghai. These branches are a carry-over from the days when the bank had a monopoly on the remittance business of South-Asian Chinese.[9] The Bank of East Asia has had its China branch in Shanghai for many years. None of these Shanghai branches are permitted to accept deposits—either in current or savings accounts—or to offer loans. These conditions may change. The Chiyu Banking Corporation is reported by various sources to have an office in Shanghai. This Hong Kong bank is, however, one of the BOC's sister banks and, thus, cannot be considered foreign.

Correspondent Banking Relations

Since 1963 the bulk of China's trade has been with non-Communist countries. With the great majority of commercial transactions being with private Western businesses, it was essential for the BOC to develop correspondent relations with Western banks. At first these were almost always subject to bilateral government-to-government clearing agreements. Those banks with Chinese branches as well as leading Hong Kong-based banks have, of course, long had correspondent accounts. Today, however, BOC correspondent relations exist between banks representing countries with whom China does not have elaborate trade agreements or settlement arrangements.

The first U.S. banks to develop correspondent relations were the Franco-American Banking Corporation of New York, in 1970, and Chase Manhattan of New York, in early 1973. David Rockefeller, president of the bank, was visiting Beijing at the invitation of the Chinese government. In reply to a question about a possible correspondent relationship, BOC officials said they saw no difficulties and would be happy to have such a relationship. The initial relationship was limited to exchanging foreign remittances, and it was not a so-called full correspondent relationship. This limited relationship was extended to a few major U.S. banks; no such bank tried to establish a full correspondent relationship until the frozen assets and related legal questions could be clarified.

First National Bank of Chicago secured an expanded correspondent relationship with the BOC in January 1978, almost a year ahead of other U.S. banks. This was in part attributed to the bank's 1977 decision to stop lending to Taiwan.[10] The new relationship permitted First National to handle commercial letters of credit, payments, collections, and foreign exchange transactions for customers. At the end of 1978, following the establishment of full U.S.-PRC diplomatic relations, First National Bank of Chicago, Citibank, and Chase Manhattan formally expanded to full correspondent relations. By March 1979 the list of U.S. correspondent banks had expanded from just three (in 1975) to ten and has since grown dramatically. By June 1980 the Bank of China confirmed it had correspondent relations with 948 foreign banks and their 2,534 branches in 142 countries and regions.[11] In mid-1981 the BOC entered into an agreement with investment bankers, Lehman Brothers Kahn Loeb, for advice by the latter on general financial matters.

FOREIGN BANK OPERATIONS IN CHINA

China recently decided that representative offices of foreign banks could be set up, especially in Beijing and Guangzhou. Representative offices and branches of foreign banks are regulated and overseen by the BOC. Chase Manhattan Bank received permission for an office during the visit of its president, Willard C. Butcher, in December 1978. Vice-Premier Li Hstien-tien informally gave the Bank of America permission to open an office in Beijing during the visit of that bank's president, A. W. Clausen. The bank announced its intention of opening a permanent representative office as soon as possible. The Bank of Tokyo opened its representative office in Beijing in early 1980, but will operate under certain undisclosed advertising limitations. The Export-Import Bank of Japan, a government agency, also opened a representative office in the capital. The Japanese finance minister approved an equivalent representative office for the BOC in Tokyo. The United Kingdom's Midland Bank became that country's first bank to announce the opening of a representative office in late 1980. In total, from 70 to 80 banks applied for licenses to open such offices by February 1981. During the first three quarters of 1981, 19 were approved (see Table 7) and a few others are likely within the year. Given the large pool of applicants and the shortage of space, China will be highly selective, probably favoring only those with a particularly close relationship or fitting in with the BOC's long-term development plans (for example, Zurich or Frankfurt).[12]

The opening of these offices and the continued expansion of representative or branch banking is completely dependent upon the Chinese requirement of reciprocity (or mutuality, as it is sometimes called) in exchanging banking services, as well as the definition the Chinese give it. China has only one bank engaged in foreign trade, the BOC, whereas the countries with which it conducts business have several private and semistate banking institutions. If China relies on a strict interpretation of the principle of reciprocity, it could limit representative offices to single-bank representatives from each country. This is not the initial practice. It is, thus, probably not a coincidence that some foreign banks should have had branches inside China, while China maintained three full-service branches outside China, with Luxembourg being recently added. As the foreign presence increases, China will press for a mutual relaxation of rules to enable its branches to be set up in cities like Paris and Tokyo. Undoubtedly, this principle will also be partially applicable to the opening of representative offices. It is also conceivable that China could

TABLE 7

Foreign Bank Representation in China, as of October 1981

Bank	Home Country	Status	City
Banca Commerciale Italiana	Italy	Representative office	Beijing
Banca Nazionale del Lavoro	Italy	Representative office	Beijing
Bank of America[a]	United States	Representative office	Beijing
Bank of East Asia	Hong Kong	Branch	Shanghai
Bank of Tokyo	Japan	Representative office	Beijing
		Liaison office	Guangzhou
Banque Nationale de Paris	France	Representative office	Beijing
		Liaison office	Guangzhou
		Liaison office	Shanghai
Barclay's Bank International	United Kingdom	Representative office	Beijing
Canadian Imperial Bank of Commerce	Canada	Representative office	Beijing
Chase Manhattan Bank	United States	Representative office	Beijing
Commerzbank	Federal Republic of Germany	Representative office	Beijing
Crédit Lyonnaise[b]	France	Representative office	Beijing
Deutsche Bank	Federal Republic of Germany	Representative office	Beijing
Export-Import Bank of Japan	Japan	Representative office	Beijing

(continued)

TABLE 7 (continued)

Bank	Home Country	Status	City
First National Bank of Chicago	United States	Representative office	Beijing
Hong Kong-Shanghai Banking Corporation	Hong Kong	Branch	Shanghai
	United Kingdom	Representative office	Beijing
Industrial Bank of Japan	Japan	Representative office	Beijing
Midland Bank	England	Representative office	Beijing
Overseas Chinese Banking Corporation	Singapore	Branch	Shanghai
		Branch	Amoy, Xiamen
Royal Bank of Canada Corporation	Canada	Representative office	Beijing
Société Générale	France	Representative office	Beijing
Standard Chartered Bank[b]	United Kingdom	Branch	Shanghai

[a]These banks were reported to be operating in Guangdong Province without having registered. British Broadcasting Corporation, Summary of World Broadcasts, November 11, 1981, quoting New China News Agency release (in Chinese) of November 5, 1981.

[b]These banks have applied to open representative offices in Guangzhou.

Sources: Banker 131 (February 1981): 15; Financial Times, February 10, 1981, p. 3, col. 6; Letter of Bank of America, People's Republic of China, Office, Hong Kong, June 3, 1981; American Banker, June 4, 1981, p. 10; British Broadcasting Corporation, Summary of World Broadcasts, October 24, 1981, p. 1; New China News Agency releases of June 27, July 9, September 5, and October 27 and 30, 1981.

link foreign bank operations with help in regaining assets of branch banks under Taiwan's control.

Several banks are moving forward from initial representative offices in Beijing or existing operations in Shanghai. The second major target area for foreign bankers is Guangdong Province and, in particular, its Shenzhen economic zone. As of late 1981, the only foreign bank given Provincial Administration approval was the Hong Kong-based Nanyang Commercial Bank. That bank is, however, a sister bank controlled by Beijing. Bank of America, Hong Kong-Shanghai Banking Corporation, and Société Générale are said, by Chinese officials, to be operating without registration or approval. Canadian Imperial Bank of Commerce and Chartered Bank have publicly stated that they are considering opening branches if the Shenzhen authorities' long-awaited banking regulations will permit branches. The local BOC branch has probably been resisting anything other than a representative office.

Banks desiring to open representative offices in China face practical difficulties. The serious shortage of office space and accommodation has thus far delayed the implementation of announced representative offices. It will be some time before the accommodation shortage is solved. Although plans for an international banking center in Beijing have twice been announced, both proposals were subsequently denied authorization, and preliminary contracts were canceled.

PROSPECTS FOR CONTINUED EXPANSION

Why are foreign banks rushing to broaden and make more permanent their presence in China? Some bankers explain this as an example of a herd mentality. Certain banks compete head-on all over the world or in particular regions. If one bank opens an office or branch somewhere, most banks in the same class will soon follow. Japanese and Canadian bankers have often commented on this trait, which they see in themselves. To a certain extent this happens even if initial profits are wafer thin or nonexistent. Generally, however, banks do analyze potential offices carefully, even if prestige and competition are given great weight. Immediate profit potential, especially with the current Chinese budget cuts, is slight. Those banks already represented have not opened offices with a view toward quick profit. Local representatives cite the following factors for their current presence: servicing existing customers trading or investing in

China, maintaining public relations with local financial organizations, preparing for the future upturn in trade, and paving the way toward full branch operations.[13]

Banks are not going to China seeking depositors. It does not have very large reserves. For all its potential, it is still a poor nation. Thus far it has not been a large borrower in terms of actual funds drawn on loans. Overhead costs will be high. The Chinese are charging enormous rents for office space and even requiring payment in full for apartments and offices two years away from completion. Costs of internal travel and meals are high by international standards. However, over the long haul, should China remain steady on the course of modernization, substantial foreign-currency financing will be required. Given its high credit rating and the shortage of similar borrowers in the world, China appears to be worth both the heavy up front costs and the required long-term commitment of resources. Foreign banks have great potential in China but do not have any chance of repeating their former influence. In the future foreign banks will, if anything, be exploited rather than be exploiters in the path of China's modernization.

NOTES

1. Yang Pei-hsin, "China's Stable Monetary System," Peking Review, June 25, 1965, p. 15.

2. William Triplett, "The Banking Industry," in Doing Business with China: American Trade Opportunities in the 1970s, ed. William Whitson (New York: Praeger, 1974), pp. 190, 194; and John Fairbank, Edwin O. Reischauer, and A. Craig, East Asia: The Modern Transformation (Boston: Houghton Mifflin, 1965), p. 630.

3. George Allen and Audrey Donnithorne, Western Enterprise in Far Eastern Economic Development: China and Japan (London: Macmillan, 1954), pp. 109, 112-14, 118.

4. Cathay Trust was controlled by Guarantee Trust of New York, International Bank of National City Bank of New York. Chase National had a substantial holding in the Chinese-American Bank of Commerce, which it later lost in the 1920s to Chinese control. Ibid., p. 109.

5. Michael L. Hunt, "Americans in the China Market: Economic Opportunities and Economic Nationalism, 1890-1931," Business History Review 51 (1977): 300-1; and Allen and Donnithorne, Western Enterprise, p. 118.

6. Economist, March 10, 1979, p. 107.

7. Charles Smith, "The Future for China's Trade," Banker 122 (February 1972): 163.

8. Allen and Donnithorne, Western Enterprise, p. 107; Y. C. Jao, Banking and Currency in Hong Kong (London: Macmillan, 1974), p. 37; and G. B. Endacott, A History of Hong Kong, 2d ed. (Hong Kong: Oxford University Press, 1973), p. 293. The unusual, for the times, local character of the bank in its early days led one historian to describe it as "the first of the British exchange banks in China to draw its capital, its direction, and its corporate status from one of the most important local centres of its sphere of operations, all the other banks in the group having been initiated in London." See also A. J. Baxter, "Origins of British Exchange Banks in China," Economic History, a supplement of Economic Journal, January 1934; and the bank's official history by Maurice Collis, Wayfoong: The Hong Kong and Shanghai Banking Corporation (London: Hong Kong Bank, 1965).

9. Dick Wilson, "Overseas Chinese Banking Corporation," Banker 126 (December 1976): 1468-70.

10. See background article in Business Week, October 17, 1977, p. 36. For a detailed account of First Chicago's link, see

Jane Tripp Howe, "First Chicago's Banking Relationships with China," East Asian Executive Reports 2 (November 1980): 5-6.

11. Chang Yen-nian, "Financing Possibilities," in China's New Economic Strategies (Switzerland: Zentrum für Unternehmungsfuhrung [Economic Management Center], 1980), p. 124. For earlier figures, see Wall Street Journal, February 8, 1979, p. 6, col. 4; and December 28, 1978, p. 2, col. 1. Further details are available in Martha Avery and William Clarke, "The Sino-American Commercial Relationship," in Chinese Economy Post-Mao, U.S., Congress, Joint Economic Committee, vol. 1 (Washington, D.C.: Government Printing Office, 1978), p. 760.

12. Banker 131 (February 1981): 15.

13. See interviews in Financial Times, February 10, 1981, p. 3, col. 8.

4

FINANCING PRACTICES AND RECENT DEVELOPMENTS

China's reputation in world markets prior to 1978 was in large part based on the remarkable fact that it was predominantly a cash trader. This conservative financial strategy was one aspect of a broader theme of self-reliance under which use of foreign goods and technology could be justified as temporary steps on the road to economic independence, but the use of foreign funds—credit—was thought to be ideologically impossible. Even the suggestion of borrowing was to be rejected on the strongest grounds because of its association with the political and economic manipulation attached to foreign loans before the Revolution.[1]

There was a great deal of truth to this perception. China came very close, although not always and not totally, to being a cash trader. Foreign credit was rarely and only indirectly tapped from 1949 through 1979. Most credit was in the form of suppliers' credit and, thus, took place without direct commercial bank borrowing.* This enabled the country to appear free of foreign debt and finance

---

*Although note the evidence of direct borrowing, including mortgages, cited in Chapter 2 under the Bank of China's history in Singapore.

charges. The policy was possible because Chinese trade surpluses were strong enough to generate sufficient foreign exchange reserves, so that direct debt could be avoided. This chapter outlines the traditional techniques used by China to finance its trade and traces the transformation from cash to indirect to direct borrowing. The philosophical and policy implications of the transformation are discussed in Chapter 6.

CASH PURCHASES

China has largely been known as a cash buyer since shortly after the Revolution. Between 1958 and 1971 China paid cash for virtually all foreign purchases. Even though there is some dispute as to the exact time when China started to arrange some short-term or deferred-payment arrangements, cash purchases of major items were continuing in the early 1970s (for example, ten Boeing 707s for U.S. $125 million, two RCA satellite ground stations, and large U.S. and Canadian grain purchases were all either cash or very short-term payouts).[2]

BARTER

Transactions based on barter are not unusual in Chinese trade. The Chinese prefer to use the terms <u>countertrade</u> or <u>counterpurchase</u>. Indeed, it appears that China's largest trade deal, the recently negotiated Sino-Japanese Trade Agreement, is based if not on a formal barter, then on barter principles—the Japanese companies buying Chinese crude, thereby giving China the paper credit with which to buy Japanese exports.[3] Older examples of barter have included a British electric company and an Italian rubber enterprise. The Italian transaction took place on the authority of the Italian Ministry of Foreign Trade in February 1963 and involved the sale of U.S. $2.2 million worth of rubber in exchange for a corresponding import of 49 different food products, including U.S. $100,000 worth of shelled eggs.[4] It has also been used in the case of Australian and Canadian grain sales to China.

Although barter has been used, it has not, for obvious reasons, proved popular with China's customers. While used sporadically in the past, and in a substantial way in relation to trade with Japan, it is unlikely to be of great importance within the next few years. However, it can be expected to grow should China run into substantial foreign exchange difficulties and, at the same time, be unwilling to cut back on imports. Several trading companies have emerged as prospective brokers, advertising their abilities as intermediaries to arrange third-party sales of goods received in barter from China.

TRADITIONAL TRADE FINANCING

Letter-of-Credit Financing of Imports and Exports

Traditionally, China's business transactions with Western firms have been cash transactions paid through letters of credit. Although certain variations have recently occurred, the use of letters of credit still predominates. The Chinese have not formally accepted the Uniform Customs and Practice for Documentary Credits of the International Chamber of Commerce (UCP). They do appear to recognize and use these customs, but with deviations that are potentially significant.[5] Chinese banking officials confirmed this unofficial acceptance of the UCP to the author in January 1980. At the very least, their practice is in broad harmony with generally accepted international practice, and the trend has been toward greater compliance with the UCP. U.S. bankers interviewed by the author characterized Chinese letters of credit and practices involved in handling them as up to international standards, if not exactly conforming, and generally involving "clean" documentary credits.

The following description of letter-of-credit financing for import and export trade is based on the author's interviews with both Chinese and foreign bankers and traders, examination of standard-form contracts widely used in trade with China, and published commentaries.* It is important when considering Chinese practice to recall that China has not formally adhered to the UCP.

---

*These are experiences of U.S. firms in the mid to late 1970s. Recent practices are becoming more liberal, but no clear patterns have yet emerged. The practices described here closely parallel those of other nations, so that it appears that China has not been discriminatory in its letter-of-credit financing practices. See the similar arrangements described in a series of studies of bilateral trade prac-

Exports from China

When China is the seller, its standard-form contracts state that payment must be by confirmed, irrevocable, divisible, and assignable letter of credit issued by a bank with which the Bank of China (BOC) has a correspondent relationship.[6] Moreover, the letter of credit must be payable through sight drafts as soon as the Chinese exporter presents the shipping documents in China to the BOC. The terms of the credit must permit partial shipments and transshipments. China's Foreign Trade Corporations (FTCs) normally require the importer to arrange for its bank to confirm the credit, thereby guaranteeing payment to the Bank of China if the documents conform to requirements.

Up until 1975, payment clauses usually required payment in renminbi (RMB). This effectively required the buyer's bank to purchase RMB from the BOC in order to pay China. The buyer was unable to know in advance of the date the credit was drawn upon what the rate of exchange would be and, hence, what price he would pay. After 1975 it has been possible to hedge against this exchange risk by buying forward from the Bank of China for several major currencies.[7] Chinese FTCs have increasingly been willing to sign contracts based on U.S. dollars or other foreign currencies. Since late 1979 most contracts for trade with China no longer use RMB as the medium of payment.

Exports to China

The standard payment clause in purchase contracts differs remarkably from that in sales contracts, where letters of credit must be confirmed and drafts drawn under them be made payable upon the presentation of shipping documents. A typical payment clause in a purchase contract, where China is importing, reads as follows:

> The Buyers, upon receipt from the Sellers of the delivery advice specified in Article 14 hereof, shall, in 15-20 days

---

tices for West Germany, Denmark, Italy, and Japan, in Victor Li, Law and Politics in China's Foreign Trade (Seattle: University of Washington Press, 1977); and various chapters in China Trade: Prospects and Perspectives, ed. David C. Buxbaum, Cassondra B. Joseph, and Paul D. Reynolds (New York: Praeger, 1982).

> prior to the date of delivery, open an irrevocable Letter of Credit with the Bank of China, in favor of the Sellers, for an amount equivalent to the total value of the shipment. The Credit shall be payable against presentation of draft drawn on the opening bank and the shipping documents specified in Article 13 hereof. The Letter of Credit shall be valid until the 15th day after the shipment is affected.[8]

As a buyer, China generally refuses to permit any of its letters of credit to be confirmed, and these credits are always issued by the BOC. The BOC issues an irrevocable sight letter of credit when the foreign exporter notifies it that the shipment is ready. Such notification would normally be transmitted by the exporter's bank. The BOC's credits are on their face transferable, but sight drafts must be drawn directly on the BOC, effectively limiting negotiation of documents to the drawee bank.

China's letter-of-credit practices are asymmetrical, in that both export and import letters of credit are to be "negotiated" at a branch of the BOC inside China. Given this provision and Chinese insistence on the right to inspect the goods upon arrival before payment, there is some authority for saying that these provisions make Chinese letters of credit merely promises to pay rather than irrevocable obligations.[9]

The effect on the BOC of requiring direct negotiation is that once the seller has shipped the goods and lost control over them, it must also arrange for the documents to be presented in, for example, Beijing without the benefit of having a local confirming bank to which it can turn for immediate payment. Therefore, the seller has temporarily lost control of the goods and documents.

China's refusal to permit a Western bank close to the Western exporter to confirm the credit also takes away one of the main advantages of documentary credits. A local confirming bank is more than security for a worried exporter. It can play an active role in dispute avoidance and, if it becomes necessary, guarantee satisfaction to the exporter. Because several people make entries on the many documents in the export process, it is possible for minor or irrelevant discrepancies to occur. These negotiations are facilitated where one bank is dealing with another bank as the intermediary. Without a confirming bank intermediary, the exporter or his banker must negotiate alone by transcontinental telex. Furthermore, such unconfirmed credits "have the grave disadvantage that they do not localize the performance of the contract of sale in the seller country. If the correspondent bank refuses to pay on tender of the document, the seller might be compelled to institute proceedings overseas—a situation that defeats the main purpose of the commercial credit."[10] However, it must be emphasized that to date this has not presented problems in actual practice for China traders.

Finally, payments from the BOC may not reach the exporter for up to 20 days from the shipment date. Without immediate local payment, the exporter is extending interest-free credit to the Chinese importer. Some German exporters dealt with this situation by merely arranging for their banks to confirm the credit without the BOC's approval or request. Reportedly, Chinese bankers have done no more than voice their complaint at this practice.[11] There cannot be many bankers willing to follow this lead. An unrequested confirmation of a BOC credit would create a binding legal guarantee of payment to the exporter yet leave the confirming bank without contractual or other legal recourse against the BOC or the exporter. Neither would the BOC's nonpayment legally permit the confirming bank to attach the BOC's account with it, an event guaranteed to invite swift reciprocal action and ruin the confirming bank's reputation with the BOC.

The BOC's reluctance to permit confirmation of its credits may be explained partly in terms of prestige. Its attitude has long been that an irrevocable letter of credit issued by the BOC is as good as an irrevocable, confirmed letter of credit issued by a leading Western bank. This was the basic attitude presented to the author in his interviews with Chinese banking officials. Their blunt answer was that a BOC letter of credit needs no confirmation. However, the attitude may also be explained in terms of the cost. Western banks will often charge a fee (for example, one-eighth of 1 percent) to confirm a credit, which the cost-conscious BOC prefers to avoid.

As previously mentioned, some Chinese letters of credit call for inspection of the goods upon arrival by the local branch of the Chinese Commodities Inspection Bureau. This delays payment and creates a theoretical problem in the legal status of documentary credits. Actual practice, however, has resulted in no significant payment disputes, and the Chinese have never been accused of improperly dishonoring a letter of credit.[12]

If the terms described for trade financing are unacceptable to an exporter with strong bargaining power, it may be possible to obtain an agreement that the documents will be negotiated in London or Hong Kong through the local branch of the exporter's bank. Alternatively, the U.S. exporter soon may be able to purchase export credit insurance from the U. S. Foreign Credit Insurance Association (FICA) or use the insurance available to exporters in other nations by arranging the transaction through a subsidiary in that country. In early 1979 private political risk insurance up to U. S. $11 million per transaction became available from the American International Group. Export insurance was already available in France and the United Kingdom.

Acceptances

Bankers' acceptances of drafts drawn under letters of credit have been used but only play a small role in trade financing.[13] Under an acceptance credit the exporter to China draws a draft on the opening bank, the advising bank, or some third bank. This draft is then accepted by the bank upon which it is drawn in exchange for the documents, leaving the exporter or his bank free to negotiate the accepted draft (for example, sell the draft at a discount to a commercial bank and, thus, obtain funds early, while hopefully transferring the risk of nonrepayment to the bank).[14]

Several Chinese letter-of-credit practices reduce the likelihood that this technique could be used. As seen above, standard-term contracts with Chinese Foreign Trade Corporations require that the letter of credit be drawn without recourse, and many acceptance banks will not accept drafts so drawn. Similarly, the FTCs generally restrict the credit so as to be issued by the BOC without an advising bank and require negotiation of drafts at a branch within China. These measures cut down the possibilities of acceptance and negotiability. Moreover, BOC credits are normally open for short time limits—usually a month or less. This reduces the time for acceptance and negotiation and, thus, the duration of credit.

Nonetheless, this technique proved useful in the financing of grain imports in 1973 and 1974. Those contracts called for time drafts, which the exporter drew against the BOC. The BOC accepted the drafts and forwarded the acceptances to the exporter, who was able to sell them at a discount to other banks.

Usuance

China's bankers have often managed to arrange regular extensions of the dates upon which bills are presented to banks for payment. Called usuance, this device is used frequently by China in its trade with Japan.[15] Usuance letters of credit (that is, payable according to their terms, say 30 or 60 days after presentation) are quite normal in international trade. However, longer periods are much less common. In the 1970s Chinese traders asked for and received as much as 180 days usuance for both imports and exports. Owing to a scarcity of foreign exchange in 1974, the amount involved reached $300 million outstanding and presented problems for Japanese suppliers. The explanation given for recent use of this facility, particularly in relation to steel, is that, while such deferred payment terms are very rare, in the case of Japan's steel industry they were linked to "facilitating China's payment in view of recent deterioration of China's foreign exchange reserve."[16] With further balance-of-payment deficits from 1979 through 1981, usuance has continued and on occasion has been substituted where original contracts had called for sight-draft payment.

Progress Payments and Deferred Payments

Even in relation to turn-key contracts negotiated in the early 1970s (for example, fertilizer or steel plants), the cash-payment practice largely continued, although the huge prices for complete plants required a modification.[17] Typically, the standard cash terms called for a down payment of 20 to 30 percent of the contract paid in two parts: advance payment at the time of signing and the balance down payment at an agreed-upon date thereafter but <u>prior</u> to the first shipment.[18] The 60 to 70 percent balance would be paid upon shipment (or in part upon partial shipment, as determined by the invoice value of each partial shipment of equipment). Further, 5 percent would be paid upon assembly of the delivered equipment, which had satisfied inspectors, and a final 5 percent after expiration of the performance guarantee or test period.[19] An example of such a clause is found in the RCA Global Communications contract with the China National Machinery Import or Export Corporation in 1972.

Deferred-payment arrangements are not always clearly distinct from progress payments. When distinguishable, deferred-payment arrangements typically require no advance down payment (or, if so, only 10 percent), but merely allow cash payments to be spread over a period of several years in regular equal installments. Frequently, a grace period is provided before installment payments begin. Reportedly, the purchase of U.S. $1.2 billion worth of complete plants ordered in 1973 (presumably fertilizer plants supplied by Pullman-

Kellogg) followed this general pattern.[20] Substantial initial payments were imposed, with the balance of U.S. $800 million payable over five years after a three-year grace period. Reportedly, no interest was directly charged, but the sellers presumably calculated interest in setting their price. Some other deferred-payment contracts expressly listed interest charges, which could be avoided by accelerated payment. Of equipment imports totaling U.S. $2.5 billion from 1971 to 1976, 60 percent were on deferred-payment terms;[21] and with large purchases or long payment periods, such as Pullman-Kellogg's six fertilizer plants, China must have entailed substantial financing costs. Initially, Chinese buyers did not concern themselves with the issue of how the supplier was financing his manufacturing and sale terms. Chinese financial planners knew quite well that interest was being paid. Gradually, the Chinese were forced to acknowledge and formally participate in the arrangement of suppliers' credits from national export agencies or banks. Often BOC guarantees were required. It is not possible to strictly separate deferred-payment arrangements from suppliers' credits, as the two are usually identical.

Suppliers' Credit

The various short- and medium-term payment devices described thus far were generally sufficient to supplement straight cash transactions. However, the leadership's decision in the early 1970s to increase capital-equipment imports required hard-currency credit facilities. These were provided by suppliers' credits of three- to five-year periods in which the supplier/exporter was asked to provide the credit needed to finance the purchase, the costs of which would be built into the purchase price.

Because the interest charged was calculated in the price, suppliers' credits were not viewed by the Chinese as a debt incurred to the foreign exporter. This was true even when China participated in the negotiations for credit. On the surface China could still proclaim its freedom from foreign debt and interest payments to capitalist bankers. But inevitably banks became involved in such transactions, either under national export credit schemes or as refinancers without recourse on the supplier's obligation. Furthermore, the financing fees paid were often higher than those that could have been secured had a direct loan to the Chinese importer been arranged. The knowledge that direct credits would often be cheaper was a significant factor several years later when political winds had sufficiently changed to enable planners to propose a switch to buyer's credits.

During the 1970s Japan had the most experience with suppliers' credits arranged openly and with Chinese participation. Some experience was gained from 1961 to 1964 when China utilized somewhat less than U.S.$1 billion in suppliers' credits. After the 1971 decision to increase trade from the U.S.$4 billion to U.S.$5 billion level to U.S.$10 billion in 1973, China started to extensively use medium-term suppliers' credits.[22] From the mid-1970s most major orders were financed on a five-year basis at 5.5 percent per annum, rising to 7.5 percent in 1975 contracts. The contracts were arranged through Japan's Export-Import (Ex-Im) Bank. Examples were a loan of ¥7.6 billion to Toyo Engineering and Mitsui to finance the sale of a urea plant valued at ¥13.6 billion. The suppliers paid 6 percent interest over a five-year term.[23] Some commercial-bank credit was also required, with the Chinese importer paying 20 to 25 percent in down payments. Another example was a March 1973 contract for the purchase of a vinylon plant, payment to be £10.66 million, with the bulk of funds provided by the Ex-Im Bank of Japan.[24]

The Bank of China also took an active role, because most government export credit agencies, like Japan's Ex-Im Bank, require the importer/buyer's national government's participation. According to one source, the BOC became a guarantor of the loan to the supplier. Both formal guarantees and the BOC endorsement of the notes for the deferred amount were used. By the end of 1973 the BOC had issued U.S.$3 billion in guarantees.[25] However, Chinese bankers denied that BOC guarantees had been used at that time, pointing out that all such contracts would, during those years, have been concluded by FTCs. Being state owned and backed, just like the BOC, their promise to pay was fully backed by the central government, and nothing would, therefore, be gained by a BOC guarantee.

Compensation Trade

In order to acquire technology without expending foreign exchange, Chinese traders have made use of what commercial lawyers call a financing buyer arrangement. In the case of China, the popular term is compensation trade. Under these arrangements the Chinese purchaser of plant and machinery provides local labor and land. The seller of technology is paid with the plant's products. Compensation agreements may call for partial or full payment in the form of output by the newly constructed plant or equipment.

The emergence of compensation trade is linked to the USSR. The compensation trade or payback schemes that China uses are modeled on development plans carried out by Lenin and Stalin in the USSR during the 1920s, arrangements now little used by that country. The failure of the USSR to continue these arrangements has been noted within China, where it is felt that this fact has contributed toward the large Soviet foreign debt. The Chinese are wary of debt on the scale of the USSR and intend to encourage such compensation-trade arrangements in order to reduce China's need to borrow.[26]

Many compensation-trade arrangements entered into are typified by a contract between Boston's Prestige Sportswear, Oxford Industries, and a Chinese enterprise. The companies provided textile finishing machines for China, which will pay for the machinery with textiles finished over an agreed period of time. This technique permits China to rapidly improve the quality and marketability of its products without spending scarce foreign exchange. The National Council for U.S.-China Trade and its counterparts in Japan and Europe are attempting to facilitate Chinese requests for further compensation arrangements. The device can also be used to acquire simple, nontechnological export industries and markets. The author visited one such operation—a clothing plant making Gloria Vanderbilt jeans. The sewing machines and other equipment were to be paid for over a ten-year period, after which the plant could continue to sell the jeans to the same Hong Kong distributor. Similar arrangements were made to increase the supply of fresh milk to Hong Kong; cows and milking machines were provided in return for milk.

The growth of these arrangements has been phenomenal. In Shenzhen, adjacent to Hong Kong, 600 contracts for compensation trade or joint production/assembly were concluded by April 1981.[27] The U.S. Department of Commerce, Bureau of East-West Trade, has predicted that such agreements will have a major impact on Chinese exports by 1985. Clearly, these arrangements have also proved to be a major avenue for foreign investment in China; approximately 422 such projects were in place by mid-1981.[28]

The BOC plays an active role in these arrangements. The business department of the BOC arranges guarantees for the foreign participant. For example, in the above-mentioned jean factory, the Hong Kong businessmen secured a BOC guarantee of production for the required number of jeans equivalent to the cost of the sewing machines within a ten-year period. If products received in Hong Kong were not sufficient at the end of the ten-year period, then the BOC would pay the difference. The guarantee agreement did not call for periodic payments but, rather, only a final payment at the end of the compensation agreement. In this regard, it differs from the guarantees offered by banks throughout the world in transactions calling for annual production minimums.

The BOC has detailed its role in processing and compensation trade contracts as follows:

1. The promotional and supervising role: Bank of China will assist the Chinese corporation in concluding foreign deals . . . it will urge them to comply with the terms of contract regarding quality, quantity and date of repayment. . . .
2. The bridging role of settlement of accounts: The Bank will adopt conventional methods of payments, . . . facilitate receipts and payments of foreign exchange. . . .
3. The financing role: . . . checking the corporation's ability to repay . . . adopt methods of Credit Guarantee, Letters of Credit, . . . loans. . . .
4. The role of trade credit information: . . . assist [with] information and market surveys . . . establish links between internal conditions and external situations. . . .
5. The advisory role in signing contracts with foreign firms: Regarding major contracts and those requiring bank guarantee or the bank acting as a witness, the Bank should participate in negotiations and study the proposed terms, so that . . . [they] will be in tune with the Government's foreign policy and the principle of equality and mutual benefit.[29]

The BOC has described the four types of payment provisions in which it participates in compensation trade as follows:

1. Commercial Credits: BOC issues a letter of guarantee for repayment of a loan from the foreign firm (seller of equipment) to the Chinese firm (buyer/user).
2. Bank Credits: Where a foreign bank lends to the Chinese firm BOC guarantees the repayment of the loan drawn under a buyer's credit against the foreign bank's letter of guarantee ensuring the foreign firm's fulfillment of their obligation to purchase the Chinese firm's output.

3. Deferred Payments: Where the Chinese firm sells the output independently and uses the proceeds to repay the foreign equipment supplier BOC will issue a guarantee and accept bills of exchange.
4. Hire Purchase: BOC will issue a guarantee covering the supplier's risk that Chinese firm will not apply to export sufficient output to meet the H-P payments.[30]

These policies were unchanged as of May 1981.

POLICY SHIFT TOWARD BUYER'S CREDITS AND LOANS

The systems of deferred payments and suppliers' credit described above are in reality forms of medium-term credit to China. It was China to which the lenders were looking for repayment. It was a borrower in all but name. The fact was implicitly acknowledged in the January 1973 statement of the minister of foreign trade, in which he stated that balance-of-payments problems required "borrowing," but this represented no fundamental change in policy. Trade could be balanced over a longer period, whereas before it had been done within each year.[31]

The closest step to direct borrowing in the mid-1970s was the establishment of mutual deposit accounts. This practice, whereby banks accept deposits from each other, is widespread in international finance. In China's case the amount on deposit with the BOC vastly exceeded the BOC's deposits with foreign banks.[32] The interest payable on the excess deposits represented the "loan" costs, and the rate was similar to that for Eurodollar interbank deposits. Mutual deposits were often arranged by or at the urging of a supplier of equipment to the Chinese. The deposits are offshore, that is to say that foreign banks deposit their funds with the Hong Kong or London branches of the BOC. In the mid-1970s Japanese surplus mutual deposits denominated in dollars or pounds were themselves financed by Japanese bank borrowing. This created problems for the borrowing banks, because the rate at which they had to borrow in order to deposit the funds with the BOC might often have a margin of profit that was too thin or nonexistent. But apparently some Japanese banks were willing to be lenders in hopes of intangible returns, such as special considerations in future dealings when China directly approached credit markets in the future.

The BOC's Annual Report for 1973 reflected this practice when its interbank deposits were listed as U.S. $2 billion—up more than 25 percent from the previous year—and U.S. $2.5 billion in 1974, although these figures are partially offset by BOC's deposits abroad and mixed in with FTC deposits with the BOC.

Such deposits were just another thinly disguised form of credit, but because funds were placed directly with China, the cost of borrowing was probably less than if done through suppliers' credits. This development is also significant, because it involved direct interbank dealings and enabled foreign banks to work and become more familiar with the BOC. The great escalation in trade by the mid-1970s, with its deficits and consequent drain on reserves, made it extremely difficult for China to continue financial policies limited to cash payments, progress payments, and deferred payments, with only occasional medium-term credits. Promoting exports, export-oriented industries, and compensation trade could only be a limited and long-term solution.

These developments did not go unnoticed by the international banking community. Indeed, more than a little interest was aroused. Speculation focused on when, not if, China would change its policy against foreign loans. Bankers' interest was stimulated anew by the possibilities presented in Vice-Premier Deng's speech in the spring of 1978.[33] His scheme to propel China into an era of modernization would obviously require massive amounts of capital. Completion of the famous Four Modernizations envisaged in his speech—involving agriculture, industry, science and technology, and national defense—required increases in capital imports that could not, within the time frame then set, be met by any foreseeable medium-term export policy. That was obvious to even the traditional ideologists among the leadership. China was pressed hard to adopt a more flexible financing policy in its own best interests, and obviously, such a change would require some reinterpretation of the doctrine of self-reliance described in the next chapter.

NOTES

1. Roger Shields, Paul Spooner, and Sandi Summerlin, "Financing Sales to China," in A New Look at Legal Aspects of Doing Business with China, ed. Howard M. Holtzman and Walter Sterling Surrey (New York: Practising Law Institute, 1979), p. 409.

2. Victor Li, "Trade with China: An Introduction," in Law and Policies in China's Foreign Trade, ed. Victor Li (Seattle: University of Washington Press, 1971), p. 6; and Edward Neilan and Charles R. Smith, The Future of the China Market (Washington, D.C.: American Enterprise Institute for Public Policy Research, 1974), p. 48.

3. The agreement was reproduced in China Business Review 6 (March-April 1978): 46-47; and in International Legal Materials 17 (1978): 6.

4. Neilan and Smith, Future of the China Market, p. 48.

5. David L. Denny, "International Finance in the People's Republic of China," in China: A Reassessment of the Economy, U.S., Congress, Joint Economic Committee (Washington, D.C.: Government Printing Office, 1975), p. 661. For further information on China's practices, see U.S., Department of Commerce, Financial Practices in United States-China Trade, prepared by David Denny and Metson (Overseas Business Reports, no. 74-64), 1974. Note also that some Communist countries have adopted these rules. See I. Mezernics, Law of Banking in East-West Trade (New York: Oceana, 1973), pp. 149-51.

6. Katherine Schwering, "Financing Imports from China," United States-China Business Review 1 (1974): 36-40; Gene T. Hsiao, The Foreign Trade of China: Policy, Law, and Practice (Berkeley and Los Angeles: University of California Press, 1977), p. 145; and Frank Münzel, "Ways of Payment in Foreign Trade," in Law and Policies in China's Foreign Trade, ed. Victor Li (Seattle: University of Washington Press, 1971), pp. 271-86. See also Deidra Dreamer, "Understanding the Bank of China's Letter of Credit Practices," East Asian Executive Reports 1 (November 1979): 3, 19-20.

7. See Chapter 1 for details of China's foreign exchange rules and procedures. The text of the controls is reproduced in Appendix B.

8. Gene Hsiao, Foreign Trade of China, p. 145, cites the Standard Form Purchase Contract of the China National Light Industrial Products Import and Export Corporation.

9. Stanley Lubman, "Contracts, Practice and Law in Trade with China: Some Observations," in Chinese Economy Post-Mao,

U.S., Congress, Joint Economic Committee, vol. 1 (Washington, D.C.: Government Printing Office, 1978), p. 772. See also Stanley Lubman, "Sino-American Trade: Legal and Practical Problems and Prospects," in Current Legal Aspects of Doing Business with Sino-Soviet Nations, ed. James T. Haight (Chicago: American Bar Association, 1973); and Dreamer, "Understanding the Bank of China," p. 20.

10. Poul Mohr, "Trade with Denmark," in Law and Policies in China's Foreign Trade, ed. Victor Li (Seattle: University of Washington Press, 1971), p. 161.

11. Arthur A. Stahnke, "Trade with West Germany," in Law and Policies in China's Foreign Trade, ed. Victor Li (Seattle: University of Washington Press, 1971), pp. 121-41.

12. Stanley Lubman, "Trade between the United States and the People's Republic of China," Law and Policy in International Business 8 (1976): 38; idem, "Contracts, Practice and Law," p. 772; William Triplett, "The Banking Industry," in Doing Business with China: American Trade Opportunities in the 1970s, ed. William Whitson (New York: Praeger, 1974), p. 202; Gene Hsiao, Foreign Trade of China, p. 145; and Gabriele C. Reghizzi, "Legal Aspects of Trade with China: The Italian Experience," Harvard International Law Journal 9 (1968): 108.

13. Münzel, "Ways of Payment," pp. 279-83; and Shields, Spooner, and Summerlin, "Financing Sales to China," pp. 421-22.

14. Münzel, "Ways of Payment," pp. 279-83.

15. Alistair Wrightman, "How Japan Finances Trade with China," U.S.-China Business Review 2 (March-April 1975): 30; "Steel Industry Plans to Give China 150-Day Usuance for December Shipments," Japan Economic Journal, January 14, 1975, p. 4; and Denny, "International Finance," pp. 668-69.

16. Denny, "International Finance," p. 668.

17. See Hans Heymann, Jr., "Acquisition and Diffusion of Technology in China," in China: A Reassessment of the Economy, U.S., Congress, Joint Economic Committee (Washington, D.C.: Government Printing Office, 1976), pp. 714-29; "Bank of China: Still a Touch of Glamour," Financial Times, June 10, 1977, p. 29, col. 5; and Richard Fry, "China's Financing Prospects," Banker 124 (December 1974): 1490.

18. Lubman, "Contracts, Practice and Law," p. 773; and Shields, Spooner, and Summerlin, "Financing Sales to China," p. 417.

19. Heymann, "Acquisition of Technology," pp. 714-29.

20. Neilan and Smith, Future of the China Market, p. 49.

21. *Financial Times*, June 10, 1977, p. 29, col. 5.

22. Wrightman, "How Japan Finances," pp. 30-32.

23. Ibid.; and Susumu Awanohara, "When Japan Deposits, China Borrows," *Far Eastern Economic Review*, June 17, 1974, pp. 42-45.

24. *Financial Times*, June 10, 1972, p. 29, col. 5.

25. Wrightman, "How Japan Finances," p. 30; and Fry, "China's Financing Prospects," p. 1490.

26. U.S., Congress, Committee on International Relations, *A New Realism: Factfinding Mission to the People's Republic of China, July 3-13, 1978* (Washington, D.C.: Government Printing Office, 1978), p. 67.

27. See report in Kevin Rafferty, "Hong Kong and China," *Financial Times*, June 15, 1981, p. v.

28. Ibid.

29. Chang Yen-nian, "Financing Possibilities," in *China's New Economic Strategies* (Switzerland: Zentrum Für Unternehmungsfuhrung [Economic Management Center], 1980), p. 132.

30. Ibid., p. 133.

31. Washington *Post*, January 18, 1973, p. 20, col. 1.

32. *Financial Times*, June 10, 1977, p. 29, col. 5; and Susumu, "When Japan Deposits," pp. 42-45.

33. Deng's speech is reproduced in *Peking Review*, March 24, 1978, and Premier Hua's Four Modernizations speech is in ibid., March 31, 1978.

5

SELF-RELIANCE, PARTY PHILOSOPHY, AND FOREIGN LOANS

Despite its revolutionary radicalism Chinese society remains remarkably conservative in most ways, including the conduct of its financial affairs. As indicated in the previous chapter, the predominating principle of domestic development and foreign trade is self-reliance. All foreign trade and almost all investment is carried out under exclusive state control, because it is considered necessary to China's ongoing efforts to ensure independence and a high degree of self-sufficiency. The linking of financial planning and trade to China's political independence is historically of the utmost significance. Only when seen in this perspective can the recent changes in policy be reconciled with China's historic avoidance and dislike of trade and investment contacts with foreign "imperialists."

The fundamental principle motivating past and present trade policy remains unchanged. The sole purpose of trade and foreign investment is to enable China to become more self-reliant.[1] Until just a few years ago it had been assumed, and often trenchantly restated, that from this principle other traditional Chinese policies followed naturally.

1. China does not borrow in order to finance imports (that is, China is not interested in long-term foreign financing).

2. China imports only what is essential for socialist construction (that is, no consumer goods, luxury items, or goods that can be made in China).
3. China finances imports as much as possible through exports and will try to balance trade bilaterally where possible.[2]

Those policies evolved during the Revolution itself and continued, with some important exceptions, until recently. They were most strongly expressed during the Cultural Revolution. Official comment from that era sums up and sheds light upon China's nineteenth-century experience and attitudes.

> For over a century, the imperialistic powers divided China into their spheres of influence, interfered in China's internal affairs, backed the reactionary authorities, subjected the Chinese people in revolutionary struggle to suppression, engineered civil wars among war lords, controlled China's customs, shipping and insurance, manipulated China's financial and monetary affairs, extorted privileges of running mines and factories, building railways, and engaging in inland navigation. They flagrantly plundered China's resources, policed the Chinese people and seriously disrupted the national economy. Rural areas were on the brink of bankruptcy. Its own industry was moribund. Major necessities like grain and cotton had to be imported in large quantities. China's entire foreign trade was in the hands of imperialists and their running dogs.[3]

In an important article from that period proclaiming China's lack of internal or external debts, one can sense the depth of feeling on this issue.[4] The author depicts Liu Shao-chi in the most derogatory terms ("the renagade hidden traitor and scab"), describing his willingness to borrow funds abroad as "a sinister plot to restore capitalism" and "trying in vain to take the road of relying on foreign aid for building factories . . . and thus reduce China to a colony or semicolony again."[5] Broadly speaking, these views expressed official policy up to the late 1970s.

How, then, may these traditional principles, so strongly stated within the last decade, be reconciled with recent events of medium-term borrowing in world capital markets? To answer that question requires a deeper understanding of the many reasons for the traditional conservative policy of the Chinese Communist party. Some reasons are obvious, but the most important are based on historical experience.

Throughout the nation prior to 1949 there was widespread, if not uniform, agreement that China's relationship with the international financial community had been one of suffering and suppression. While domestic bankers were often blamed, particularly for the usurious interest rates that kept the peasantry impoverished, foreign lenders were believed to be responsible for widespread political interference and manipulation, as well as the incredible inflation after World War II.

This history was repeated relatively soon after the Revolution, forcibly reminding China's leaders of the underlying wisdom of these principles. Its initially close ties with the USSR soon developed into both a wholesale patterning of Chinese institutions on the Soviet model and a remarkable degree of economic, technological, and financial dependence. Sizable Soviet loans were taken beginning in 1950.[6] A total of 52 of these loans were estimated to have accounted for 28 percent of total budgetary investment.[7]

Deteriorating relations, resulting in severed ties between the two powers, left China with severe withdrawal symptoms. The entire economy was shaken, and great strain was placed on export earnings in order to pay off the Soviet loans. One commentator summed up the effects of this bitter experience on the Communist leadership.

> China learnt what it considers a hard lesson in the late 1950s—that one should not build too great a reliance on any one nation as a trading partner. This lesson seems to have coloured its home and foreign economic policy ever since. . . . China has pursued a trade policy of buying only as much as it sells and far as possible, not allowing one supplier nation to gain overwhelming dominance. . . . [As a result] one of the hardest nuts for exporters to crack has been China's approach to credit.[8]

This hard lesson was not, however, uppermost in planners' minds in the early 1970s.

As trade rapidly expanded China took on both direct and indirect credits. With the increased integration into world markets came a degree of dependence. China had planned to increase its exports in order to meet expected trade imbalances. However, because it had become somewhat integrated, China was unable to avoid the effects of the economic recession in 1973-75.[9] The recession caused demand for its exports to drop and resulted in two years of balance-of-payments deficits (only the second time it had occurred since 1960), and reduced reserves had to be endured for three years; many plant and equipment contracts had to be canceled, and discretionary imports reduced.

The historical experience had by 1977 been largely negative: there were proved risks of foreign interference and manipulation, risks of excessive dependence on a single nation, and risks in integrating China into the world economy.[10] These real risks have frequently been weighed against the desire to modernize the economy far more rapidly. The resultant debate among planners, idealogs, and pragmatics has been controversial and personally damaging for those on the losing side. This is particularly true of the current winner, Deng Xioping, who has lost the debate twice before at great personal cost. More than anyone else, he is linked with the recent changes in economic goals and practices. In 1975 he had reshaped the definition of self-reliance to explain acceptance of deferred payment terms as being done "in the knowledge that we are capable of making regular payments. We must remain free from debts, both at home and abroad, and go not further than that."[11]

Further reinterpretation became necessary after the Four Modernization goals were announced. The potential policy change was signaled by remarks to visiting trade delegations hinting at a willingness to borrow. In August 1978, when it was already known China was negotiating for credit with several Japanese and British banks, Beijing's Kwangming Daily quoted with favor Lenin's 1921 comment on the acceptability of Communist countries letting foreigners invest capital and thereby helping to "quickly develop the socialist economy."[12] The article was accompanied by an editorial note deploring the fact that "some people [wear] mental shackles in the form of conservation . . . and blind expulsion of foreign things"; therefore, "bringing in advanced technology and foreign capital is still regarded by some people as a forbidden zone." The article was viewed as signaling the acceptability of foreign loans and joint ventures. Thus, an ideological foundation for changes in policy was established. China's foreign trade minister, Li Chiang, publicly indicated further changes in late 1978 during a Hong Kong press conference, when he stated that China would accept direct governmental loans and would welcome aid from the UN Development Programme.[13]

Indeed, attitudes toward loans have never been ideologically absolute. Just as loans from the USSR and 12-to-18-month loans for Canadian and Australian grain imports were accepted in 1970, the Chinese themselves did not object to being lenders. Other countries could take on foreign loans, and China conceded the propriety of this in its concessional lending to Tanzania, Pakistan, Sri Lanka, and Malta.[14] The important point was that independence was to be preserved. China stated that just as it did not want to be dominated, it did not intend its loans to be tools of domination. Neither was the principle of self-reliance carried out internally; provinces and local enterprises were, of course, encouraged to borrow for domestic needs. Banks have been granting loans since the Revolution, and such lending continued during the most extreme years of Moaist orthodoxy.

These ideological variations were also weighed with other factors justifying change.[15] Shifting to buyer's credits was not necessarily less expensive than suppliers' credits, but the Chinese buyer would know and could control overall financing costs. The switch would also permit the use of suppliers other than those with banks or governments willing to grant credit. Payments could be spread over longer periods. Finally, China's suppliers encouraged the switch, because it would ease their cash-flow problems and marginally reduce their assumed credit risk.

Since the policy change, many loans and lines of credit, both commercial and government-to-government, have been agreed. These are described in the next chapter. Nonetheless, China had by early 1981 showed signs of retreating somewhat to a more conservative position. China has consistently sought out noncredit alternative sources of finance, such as compensation trade, joint ventures, and barter schemes. This attitude was characterized by Vice-Minister for Foreign Trade Chin Jie, who said, "Our borrowing depends on our ability to repay, sticking to self-reliance and hard work. We can control ourselves. With deferred payment, we even pay ahead of schedule."[16] Similarly, Bu-Ming, president of the BOC, said that China planned "to absorb and make use of foreign funds in a planned way and in accordance with the principle of upholding independence and self-reliance."[17]

It must be acknowledged that China's economic policy making has generally mirrored political policy. Just as the political winds have often dramatically reversed direction, so too has the economic policy. The current policies that permit borrowing could conceivably be as easily terminated as continued.*

---

*The author wishes to make it clear that by the above he does not mean to imply that China would default on loans outstanding at the

NOTES

1. Eugene A. Theroux, "China's Foreign Trade: Principles, Institutions, and Performance," in Post-Mao China and U.S.-China Trade, ed. Shao-chuan Land (Charlottesville: University Press of Virginia, 1977), p. 58.

2. Ibid., p. 78.

3. Ibid., p. 55. Chou Hua-min, addressing the United Nations Conference on Trade and Development in Santiago, Chile, in 1972.

4. Tsai Ching, "Our Country Is Now a Socialist Country without Internal or External Debts," Peking Review, May 23, 1969, pp. 15-17.

5. Ibid.

6. K. Reese, "Mainland China and Western Trade Credits," Intereconomics 2 (1976): 46, 47, 49. See also David Denny, "International Finance in the People's Republic of China," in China: A Reassessment of the Economy, A Compendium of Papers, U.S., Congress, Joint Economic Committee (Washington, D.C.: Government Printing Office, 1975), pp. 653-77.

7. Audrey Donnithorne, "China's Economic System," Three Banks Review, no. 103 (September 1974), pp. 3-25. China redeemed the Soviet loans and interest of R1,406 million by 1975. Tsai Ching, "Our Country," p. 16.

8. G. Hawten, "Traders Look to Steady Rise," Times (London), March 21, 1973, p. iii.

9. Lynn Feintech, "The Role of International Trade and Finance in the People's Republic of China," in A New Look at Legal Aspects in Doing Business with China, ed. Howard M. Holtzmann and Walter S. Surrey (New York: Practising Law Institute, 1979), pp. 389-90; and Alistair Wrightman, "How Japan Finances Trade with China," U.S.-China Business Review 2 (March-April 1975): 30.

10. Feintech, "The Role of Trade and Finance," p. 390. See, however, the report of Chinese Premier Zhao Ziyang's speech in December 1981 to the National People's Congress, where he urged

---

time any change in policy occurs. If, and when, a change in policy comes, knowledge of China's past business practices and its experiences with the USSR inthe 1960s confirms the belief that China will make timely payment of loans outstanding at the time such a policy change would be made.

integration into world markets and economic links with foreign countries. Asian Wall Street Journal Weekly, December 7, 1981, p. 1.

11. David Denny, "China's Foreign Financial Liabilities," U.S.-China Business Review 2 (January-February 1975): 34.

12. Quoted in the Wall Street Journal, August 25, 1978, p. 12, col. 1; and Melinda Liu, "Financing the New Customer," Banker 128 (December 1978): 49.

13. Wall Street Journal, December 19, 1978, p. 17, col. 2; and Bureau of National Affairs, International Trade Reporter, no. 238 (January 2, 1978), p. A-6.

14. John F. Cooper, China's Foreign Aid: An Instrument of Peking's Foreign Policy (Lexington, Mass.: Lexington Books, 1976).

15. See, generally, "China: Signs of Possible Emergence," Financial Times, May 30, 1978, p. 34, col. 6.

16. Melinda Liu, "China Will Stay Cautious despite a U.S. $60 Billion Credit," Far Eastern Economic Review, October 5, 1979, p. 77.

17. Quoted in Beijing Review, February 18, 1980, p. 8.

6

INTERNATIONAL FINANCIAL REQUIREMENTS AND INTERNAL SOURCES OF FINANCE

ESTIMATES OF FINANCIAL NEEDS

During the period from 1978 to mid-1980, estimates of China's external financing of the National Economic Plan ending in 1985 were numerous, varied, and often revised. Early estimates of U. S. $200 billion were quickly discounted. China's 1982 balance-of-payments deficit was predicted to be U. S. $11. 5 billion by one bank, but Louis Saubolle of the Bank of America forecast U. S. $6 billion. [1] Foreign financing requirements were predicted variously to range from U. S. $30 billion to U. S. $60 billion between 1980 and 1985. [2] The wide variety of rough estimates was caused by the lack of firm data and, hence, were more educated guesses than estimates. Although most estimates had by early 1980 settled in the U. S. $35 billion-to-U. S. $50 billion range (including joint venture investment inflows), *

---

*Chinese officials stated that these figures were too high for credits taken as loans. The figures are only correct if other inflows of foreign exchange, such as those from joint ventures and compensation-trade agreements, were included in the total. However, the officials indicated that even this estimate could be higher if "things

China scrapped its 1978 plan in June 1979 at the Fifth National People's Congress. Once again China's initial plans for radical economic transformation had proved unworkable. However, unlike the Great Leap Forward and the Cultural Revolution, China did not drop or reverse the program. Instead of canceling the modernization strategy and shifting to a new policy, the program was restructured. This was realistic and is now viewed by Western observers as a positive step.

While the process of readjustment had begun by mid-1980, China admitted a deficit of nearly U.S.$12 billion in a budget that was supposed to have balanced at U.S.$79.2 billion. As explained in Chapter 1 a domestic deficit impacts international financial requirements in several ways, not the least of which is China's ability to finance the local-cost portion of projects involving substantial foreign funding. Nonetheless, the vice-chairman of the State Planning Commission, Yang Bo, speaking in September 1980, said China would probably borrow more than U.S.$20 billion abroad between 1980 and 1985. Even as revised during late 1980, these figures were large enough to attract the attention of the world banking community, which as stated, was hard pressed to find qualified borrowers.[5] Further reductions in budget plans announced in 1980 and 1981 have led to a corresponding reduction in estimates of short-term borrowing requirements. Given the frequency of readjustment announcements, an estimate contained here would be quickly out of date. The press and banks, as well as U.S. government agencies, regularly report revised estimates of the international financial requirements.

INTERNAL SOURCES

Foreign bank loans are not China's only source of needed finance. Numerous sources are available, including many that can be

---

go well."[3] These figures are best understood when placed in relation to China's overall capital expenditure. In 1979 the central government announced that government investment in capital construction during fiscal 1979 would be RMB 40 billion (U.S.$26.14 billion). Local government investment would be RMB 1 billion. One expert noted that 10 percent of 1979's capital construction would be funded from overseas loans.[4] The policy on capital construction and, thus, the related figure for required foreign equipment were twice slashed, in 1980 and early 1981.

considered internal resources and are generated or collected domestically, such as overseas remittances, joint venture investment, and gold production.

China's economic planners and bankers have often expressed their plans to tap several domestic and foreign sources for financing. Domestic growth and increased productivity are the primary and ultimate sources. Export earnings are to be increased. "These funds can be accumulated through the expansion of industrial and agricultural production and development of foreign trade."[6] But all conventional methods of obtaining foreign funds, including deferred payments, borrowed funds, compensation trade, direct joint investment, and foreign aid are to be used.

Increased Export Earnings

In Chapter 1 it was pointed out that foreign trade plays a relatively small role in the economy. Although small, trade has had the historically important economic role of aiding central planners to meet unforeseen production shortfalls[7] and is still used to meet shortages in such areas as food and consumer goods. But trade expansion through export industrial growth is the sine qua non of the Four Modernizations. As first announced the export drive portion of the Four Modernization goals was to be concentrated in oil, textiles, and light manufacturing, with targets of 20 percent per annum growth to U.S. $3.3 billion by 1985.[8] This includes an estimate of U.S. $10 billion a year oil export earnings by 1985. All of these goals have been scaled down recently, or the time frame has been extended.

Despite readjustments and setbacks in economic goals, export growth has been excellent. For example, exports in 1978 were up about 29 percent over 1977 (imports up 50 percent) and increased again in 1979 by 26 percent. Oil exports, however, were particularly disappointing. In terms of gross tonnage, oil has stagnated and is presently in a decline. Only increases in world oil prices kept the volume up. The World Bank's study on China's oil sector predicts stagnation in production through 1985 and an actual decline in exports owing to increased and grossly inefficient domestic consumption. Until recently, China had generally maintained a surplus in its visible trade balances and presumably had always had a surplus on invisibles—the latter owing to practices that preserved most shipping and insurance for itself in both import and export trade. The shock of deficits in 1978-80 caused leaders to shift away from imports, cancel projects, and emphasize exports. The overall effect was designed not merely to reduce the deficit but to restore a real surplus in visible balance of trade.

China's export plans have run into several real snags. First, import requirements for nondevelopmental purposes have been far greater than planned. Grain imports were planned at the level of 5 million to 6 million metric tons (mmt) a year. This goal has been exceeded every year since 1978. Imports have been about 10 mmt per year. In the 12 months ending May 1981 they reached 15.5 mmt.[9] With persistent reports of drought-induced crop failures in two major provinces, grain imports are likely to climb much further, although foreign aid requested for famine relief during 1981 may pay for the increase. China has made a commitment to buy 6 mmt of grain from the United States alone for several years.

The second problem area is energy reserves. They are believed to be enormous, though estimates of reserves vary significantly.[10] Many offshore wells have been successful in 1981 and confirmed predictions about reserves. However, extraction and use are limited by the availability of capital and changeability of policy. While China has recently been a significant exporter of oil and coal, hoped-for increases will require substantial lead time, as well as massive and sustained capital investment.[11] Oil and coal exports were to have been increased in 1978 and 1979; oil production advanced less than 2 percent in 1979 and not at all in 1980 (see Table 8). In early 1981 the government officially revised oil and coal production targets downward. Similarly, coal production was dramatically below goals, up only 0.03 percent, and was projected to be 20 to 30 percent short of the 1985 goals. To cover the lead time needed to significantly increase exports, China will need longer and larger credits than the small amount of five-to-ten-year credits used prior to 1981; but leaders are highly ambivalent about making the needed investment because of planning mistakes in other industries and a general reluctance to borrow at commercial rates.

Specifically in relation to petroleum, there were many contributing factors. Goals were overambitious and failed to allow for the lead time necessary to bring offshore oil on stream. Policy makers also differed over investment priorities (onshore versus offshore), the degree of foreign participation, and the need to encourage conservation by cutting back development of nonrenewable fuel resources. An offshore oil rig disaster led to a dislocating shakeup among petroleum ministry officials. The long-awaited petroleum law had not been finalized by early 1981. The resultant shortage has created a

TABLE 8

Estimated Chinese Crude Oil Production and Exports, 1970-80

Year	Metric Tons (millions)	Barrels per Day (thousands)	Exports (millions of metric tons)
1970	28.2	564	—
1975	74.5	1,490	—
1977	93.6	1,872	11.0
1978	104.0	2,080	11.2
1979	106.1	2,120	13.0
1980	105.8	2,100	12.0

Sources: A. A. Meyerhoff, "China's Petroleum Industry," in China Trade: Prospects and Perspectives, ed. David C. Buxbaum, Cassondra E. Joseph, and Paul D. Reynolds (New York: Praeger, 1982); Far Eastern Economic Review, January 30, 1981, p. 44; and March 6, 1981, pp. 41-42.

large gap in promised deliveries to Japan. Luckily, this happened during the 1980-81 world market glut.

Had petroleum production and exports kept pace with 1978-79 plans, China could well have avoided most of its 1980 and 1981 balance-of-payments deficit. The factors listed above do not really explain why this sector of the economy is being left stagnant. Possibly production problems are more fundamental and severe than generally thought.[12] For the medium term, oil has tremendous potential as a source of foreign exchange, and developments in this section will be closely watched by those interested in China's financial condition. Some encouragement can be found in the drilling contracts signed in late 1980 and early 1981. Some foreign companies, as well as the China National Oil Company, announced several successful offshore wells. But further drilling is required before preliminary production estimates are possible.

The recent World Bank study seems to suggest that the leadership recognized that industry was being wasteful in its energy consumption.[13] It seems to imply that oil production was not increased because to do so would promote continued energy inefficiency, but this cannot alone explain why production dropped. It would have been possible, after all, to increase production but reserve the increase for the export market. Efficiency could also be increased by charging a higher domestic price. The study cannot explain why production dropped.

The third problem area concerns international trade regulation and new measures to restructure export trade practices. Increased Chinese exports are significantly hindered by other nations' slowness to extend most-favored-nation (MFN) treatment to China. The term most favored nation is slightly misleading, as it is now the normal treatment between nations, not really a special treatment. It is abnormal for a country not to be given MFN treatment. Although the European Economic Community extended MFN treatment in 1978, Japan and the United States only did so in 1980. For quite some time the United States and China were unable to agree on textile imports, and the United States imposed a quota for a year before agreement was reached.

China faces the same nontariff barriers that all other developing nations are attempting to overcome: complex and diverse safety, labeling, shipping, and regulatory restrictions. Internally, China continues to struggle with the difficult process of selecting and adequately funding those industries to head the export drive. The varying quality standards and a lack of awareness of Western tastes have also hampered export growth. Trade problems are not limited to importing, because China presents difficulties for competitors in the developing world. Its export policy now favors industries producing products most likely to compete head on with nations like Egypt, India, and Pakistan, all of which have expressed concern over the extent to which their exports are being damaged by Chinese competition.

None of these difficulties present insurmountable obstacles. Indeed, some of them (for example, shortfall in oil production) stem from the very problems they are designed to overcome, namely, lack of sufficient foreign exchange. Other difficulties have been caused by internal problems already recognized and being tackled by China's leadership. The sheer physical size of the nation, the size of the economy, the caution of provincial administrators, and the inherent difficulties in economic central planning have forced continual reconsideration of plans and a redirection of resources. The scrapping of the original goals of the Four Modernizations, like the readjustments of 1979 and 1980, should be welcomed as signs of realism, rather than timidity or lack of commitment. With the whole economy going through a shakedown cruise, it is inevitable that export trade will feel its share of the effects.

Reserves and Production of Gold and Strategic Metals

China and its people have a historic attachment to gold as money and as decoration. Not surprisingly, China is a major world producer of gold, as well as a buyer and seller. While figures for reserves and production have not been officially published, information may become available through membership in the International Monetary Fund (IMF).

In late 1980 Yao Yilin, a vice-premier, told Japanese visitors that reserves were U.S.$6 billion. It is generally believed by Japanese and British observers that three-fourths of this total was in gold (equivalent to 230 tons). In 1970 reserves had been estimated at U.S.$720 million of which U.S.$560 million was in gold.[14] China's decision to start publishing monetary statistics once again revealed gold holdings to be 12.3 million troy ounces at year-end 1980.

During the 1960s the U.S. Bureau of Mines estimated production at approximately 50,000 troy ounces per year. More recent figures give a range of from 25 to 60 tons a year.[15] Consolidated Gold Fields, after teams visited China in 1979, estimated production at from 30 to 60 tons a year. At these levels China rivals Canada as the world's third largest producer, which would be worth U.S.$1.05 billion per year assuming an average price of U.S.$650 an ounce.[16] Recent gold prices have been much lower. Several reports of new gold finds have been made in the Chinese press. These have largely resulted from a major mining program combined with imports of equipment, including Dutch dredgers. Gold production is widespread, discoveries being claimed in all 27 provinces and autonomous regions, but concentrated in four provinces.[17] It is accepted that production can be increased by from 50 to 100 percent by the 1990s.

China's transactions in gold are shrouded in secrecy, but this is not exceptional in world bullion markets. A few times its sales and purchases, or rumors thereof, have come to light. Sales include the following: September 1961, 7,600 ounces in London;[18] 1960s, generally substantial but unspecified quantities in Macao;[19] 1976, 80 tons of gold valued at U.S.$350 million in London;[20] and December 1976, 15 to 20 tons valued at U.S.$73 million to U.S.$100 million in London.[21]

Purchases include the following:[22] U.S.$115 million in 1965; 30 tons in 1966; 70 tons in 1968; and U.S.$20 million in 1969. To this must be added unofficial gold purchases in South Asia, possibly as high as U.S.$100 million to U.S.$300 million annually. Dealing in London has been somewhat active since 1972 and quite active since 1979. Several of the Hong Kong sister banks are active on local gold markets, most notably the Po Sang Bank.[23]

The cumulative effect of production, sales, and purchases is not known, but China appears to be a net purchaser. Certainly, considerable quantities must be consumed in dental care and industry. Purchases are spread throughout Asia and Europe, but London, Zurich, and Hong Kong (and formerly Macao) are the centers for Chinese dealings. In London the BOC's name is linked with Samuel Montagu, the merchant bank and bullion dealer.[24] Silver trade has also been noticed, and silver has been included in official reserves.[25]

As world attention in the 1980s focuses upon the importance of strategic metals,[26] China is emerging as a major exporter. It has become the major or only non-Soviet-bloc, non-South African source of many rare metals. It is known to have commercial deposits of all but 10 of the world's 140 minerals and probably leads the world in production of about 17 of them, including tungsten, titanium, and molybdenum. Other exotic exports include vanadium (expected exports in 1981 are 4,000 tons), germanium (expected 1981 exports are 7 tons or about 6 percent of Western consumption), and rare earth oxides, such as europium and yttrium. It is too early to assess the potential for these specialized exports.

Tourism

For many countries tourism is an extremely important source of foreign exchange income, if not the most important. China already possesses a substantial tourist and "official visitors" market and has been quick to increase income from tourism. Recent years' figures, set out in Table 9, show dramatic yearly increases.

TABLE 9

Tourism Statistics, 1977-81
(in millions)

	Receipts (in millions of U.S. dollars)	Foreign Visitors	Overseas Chinese Visitors	Hong Kong Compatriots
1977	100	n.a.	n.a.	n.a.
1978	243	n.a.	n.a.	n.a.
1979	464	n.a.	n.a.	n.a.
1980	540	0.2	0.53	5.0
1981*	146	n.a.	n.a.	2.0

n.a. = not available

*First-quarter statistics only.

Sources: Beijing Review, November 6, 1980; Ta Kung Pao, November 6, 1980; China Quarterly 83 (September 1980): 611; and Financial Times, June 1, 1981, p. 3. The latter two cite State Statistical Bureau communiqués.

These figures must be suspect, however, as the Beijing Review has given enormously varying figures throughout 1980.[27] The figures used are end-of-year totals given in early 1981. Some differences may be attributable to the definitions being used (that is, including or excluding business travelers, official delegations, and overseas Chinese). The enormous differences may be caused by the government travel agency excluding Hong Kong "compatriot" visitors from the overseas Chinese category used by the State Statistical Bureau. Unfortunately, published data does not give the definitions used.

Even if the statistics should be viewed skeptically, the tremendous potential is real and has only begun to be tapped. China has already reached physical limits on its abilities to house and transport visitors. The shortage of hotel space was obvious in 1978, but planners vacillated over the grade and number of rooms to be added, as well as the financing. Negotiations with numerous foreign hoteliers bogged down. Despite several announced preliminary agreements, few projects had been finalized, and little building had even started by 1980. Transportation facilities, particularly the jet fleet, have been quickly and systematically expanded and upgraded. New techniques, such as bus and hydrofoil day tours from Hong Kong, have also been launched; these bypass the hotel-space shortage, as do cruise-ship visits. Continued large increases in income can certainly be expected for the medium term, and Bank of America in Hong Kong projects 3.5 million visitors by 1985. Several hotels started construction in early 1981. The chairman of Luxingshe (International) Hong Kong, Limited, the national tourist agency's Hong Kong subsidiary, estimated that total 1981 tourist income would reach U.S.$700 million—a rise he characterized as being only 13 percent over 1980. These November 1981 figures do not, however, fit in with the statistics shown in Table 9.

Overseas Remittances

Chinese living outside mainland China, normally referred to as overseas Chinese, and those in Hong Kong and Macao, referred to as compatriots by the PRC and as overseas Chinese by others, have traditionally remitted funds to their families in the PRC. Indeed, the transfer of these funds is one of the chief reasons why the BOC has branch offices both outside China and in the principal mainland areas from which migration abroad took place in the late nineteenth and early twentieth centuries.[28] The government has taken many measures over the last few decades to actively encourage the continuation of this practice in order to maintain its balance of payments. Recipients of foreign-currency remittances must deposit them with the Bank of China in exchange for RMB. To absorb and encourage this extra remitted income, special housing and flats in selected villages are available for dependents of overseas Chinese. Additional portions of rationed items are also available to recipients.

For investment purposes, overseas Chinese investment corporations were formed early on during communist rule. This process has been revived recently with stock and bond sales targeted overseas. A more recent innovation is the extension of new shopping services at the China Products emporium in Hong Kong, where relatives can buy items for families in China. Not only will they pay as much as U.S. $500 for a color television, but the government-owned company charges 50 percent customs tax. Such sales take place in U.S. foreign exchange and, thus, help Beijing's balance of payments. New methods of attracting overseas remittances are encouraged, including issuing RMB credit cards to overseas Chinese who pay their bill with foreign exchange.[29]

Some concerns have been expressed in the past about whether or not designated recipients are actually allowed to receive and use these remittances. In 1955 the State Council ordered that officials treat dependents of overseas Chinese with consideration and in no event were they to force these recipients to enter cooperatives, place the funds in savings deposits, or purchase bonds. Nor were officials to interfere with recipients spending these funds on weddings, funerals, and other special occasions.[30] However, these regulations were much abused during the Cultural Revolution, when suspicion of all overseas links, including financial, became very intense. During 1978 past practices of extortion and persecution of families receiving such remittances were condemned, and in some instances, compensation was paid. The right of Chinese citizens to receive cash gifts from relatives overseas (free of sanctions or blackmail) has recently been stressed repeatedly throughout China. Present policy focuses on the foreign exchange benefit to the nation rather than the individual recipient, who must exchange the foreign currency at the BOC.

Various estimates have been made of the amount of income from such overseas remittances. They were estimated to be U.S. $150 million a year during the prosperous periods prior to World War II and averaged about U.S. $35 million a year from 1950 to 1960.[31] Estimates in the 1970s and 1980 ranged from U.S. $100 million to U.S. $1 billion a year. While China has not officially published totals of remittance income, the BOC did announce in 1979 that such income in 1978 was up 20 percent over 1977.[32]

Direct Investment in Chinese Industries

China announced its intention in December 1978 to permit direct foreign equity investment in joint ventures on Chinese soil, adding that conditions and regulations would be clarified later. Strictly speaking, this is not one of China's own sources. But joint ventures, like compensation trade, require Chinese investment of resources as well. Such investment projects are thus not purely foreign sources. Work began almost immediately to devise an investment code and other necessary legislation, such as patent protection and tax laws. A basic framework law on joint ventures was enacted in July 1979. That law has been examined in great detail elsewhere.[33]

The Joint-Venture Law (JVL) permitted foreign individuals or corporations to invest directly or in trust in Chinese enterprises. For each joint venture (JV) with a foreign equity participation, the establishment of a new company is required. Terms for the gradual phasing out of foreign participation must be approved in advance by the Foreign Investment Commission (FIC). In theory, foreign participants would be allowed to own up to 100 percent of the joint company for a certain time period. This would be tied to gradual reduction of equity participation leading to ultimate majority control by the Chinese. It was expected that the normal equity participation would be 51 percent Chinese and 49 percent foreign. The first joint ventures approved by the FIC were along the latter lines, but others have been 33 percent among each of three partners or 50 percent each between two.[34] The JV is governed by Chinese law and must pay taxes at special rates applicable to such companies. The government stated that priority would be given to approving those JV operations established in export industries or tourism.

Other forms of direct investment are possible through compensation trade and joint production arrangements. The latter form of investment does not necessarily involve the creation of a new enterprise nor equity participation; most such arrangements are created by simple contracts. The majority of compensation agreements, joint processing contracts, and JVs—both contractural and equity—have been with Hong Kong and Macao partners.[35] The majority are also clustered in Guangdong Province, which had, by the end of 1980, 6,380 of these kinds of contracts with overseas enterprises. Equity JVs have grown slowly and steadily: 17 were approved by the FIC by late 1980, increasing to 20 by December 1980; and 22 projects, involving a total investment of U.S.$210 million, by June 1981. The sums involved are quite modest. Contractural JVs totaled 360 in March 1981 and involved U.S.$500 million. When oil exploitation ventures and special-mining investment are added (about 25 projects), investment by foreign participants up to June 1981 has been approximately U.S.$1.5 billion to U.S.$1.6 billion.

The pattern of euphoric enthusiasm lapsing into gloom over prospects, so evident in previous peaks in China's foreign-trade plans, appeared once again in relation to joint ventures. The tremendous initial excitement and numerous announced deals gave way to pessimism over the lack of further detailed laws, regulations, and FIC approval. The first approvals of JV agreements did not come about until 12 months after the law was promulgated and involved relatively small companies in tourism. Multinational companies were very cautious as they waited for the further development of a legal infrastructure in China.[36] Some progress was made by early 1981 with the adoption of corporate and personal income tax legislation, foreign exchange regulations, labor regulations, and additional procedures for registration of JVs, but no civil or economic code seemed forthcoming at that time. Large investments are being actively considered, but practical problems in early JVs and joint production arrangements have made investors cautious.

NOTES

1. Leo Goodstadt and Pamela Clarke, "Foreign Banks and Chinese Loans: The Awakening Giant of the East," Euromoney, October 1978, pp. 68-79.

2. Bureau of National Affairs, International Trade Reporter, no. 252 (April 10, 1979), p. C-1; and Melinda Liu, "Rock-Bottom Terms Are a Must for Foreigners," Far Eastern Economic Review, September 21, 1979, p. 62.

3. Dick Wilson, "How Banks Work in China," Banker 130 (January 1980): 22.

4. Kenneth Lieberthal, "China: The Politics behind the New Economics," Fortune 100 (December 31, 1979): 49.

5. Times (London), September 29, 1980.

6. Chang Yen-nian, "Financing Possibilities," in China's New Economic Strategies (Switzerland: Zentrum für Unternehmungsfuhrung [Economic Management Center], 1980), pp. 123-33, 128-29.

7. David L. Denny, "International Finance in the People's Republic of China," in China: A Reassessment of the Economy, U.S., Congress, Joint Economic Committee (Washington, D.C.: Government Printing Office, 1975).

8. Financial Times, May 30, 1978, p. 34, col. 6; and revised later in the Far Eastern Economic Review, May 18, 1981, p. 9.

9. Financial Times, June 2, 1981, p. 27. China has signed a wheat agreement with Canada calling for sales to 8.4 to 10.5 mmt and with Australia and Argentina for another 10 mmt. The former was renewed and extended in December 1981. John Nuttall, "China's Agriculture-Related Imports: Current Status and Future Prospects," in China Trade: Prospects and Perspectives, ed. David C. Buxbaum, Cassondra E. Joseph, and Paul D. Reynolds (New York: Praeger, 1982).

10. Much of the information in the section is based on the work of Arthur A. Meyerhoff, "China's Petroleum Industry," in China Trade: Prospects and Perspectives, ed. David C. Buxbaum, Cassondra E. Joseph, and Paul D. Reynolds (New York: Praeger, 1982), and sources cited therein. Other reports are Anthony Rowley, "Cashing In on China's Oil Boom," Far Eastern Economic Review, November 14, 1980, pp. 52-54; Newsweek, October 30, 1978, p. 155; James Tanner, "Asian Bonanza," Wall Street Journal, October 19, 1978, p. 1, col. 1; and George Lauriat, "Hope beneath the Sea," Far Eastern Economic Review, March 6, 1980, pp. 41-42. The foreign policy implications are discussed by Selig Harrison, China, Oil

and Asia Conflict Ahead? (New York: Columbia University Press, 1977).

11. Edward Neilan and Charles R. Smith, The Future of the China Market (Washington, D.C.: American Enterprise Institute for Public Policy Research, 1974), p. 48; and Newsweek, April 23, 1973, p. 81. An early and excellent analysis of China's oil prospects is Nicholas Ludlow, "China's Oil," U.S.-China Business Review, vol. 1 (January-February 1974). More up to date is Meyerhoff, "China's Petroleum Industry."

12. As reported and summarized in Economist, June 20, 1981, pp. 34-35.

13. Some analysts believe production figures are exaggerated, because they argue, China does not have the refinancing capacity for claimed production in the past few years. See George Lauriat, "Hope beneath the Sea," p. 42.

14. Colina MacDougall and David Marsh, "Peking Learns the Art of Playing the Bullion Market," Financial Times, December 18, 1980, p. 4; and Dick Wilson, "The Bank of China Steps Out," Banker 124 (February 1974): 105-10.

15. William Triplett, "The Banking Industry," in Doing Business with China: American Trade Opportunities in the 1970s, ed. William Whitson (New York: Praeger, 1974), p. 199.

16. Financial Times, May 1, 1980.

17. Ibid.; Far Eastern Economic Review, January 25, 1980, p. 27.

18. Triplett, "The Banking Industry," p. 199.

19. "Bank of China: Still a Touch of Glamour," Financial Times, June 10, 1977, p. 29, col. 5.

20. Deidra Dreamer, "Recent Financial Developments in China," East Asian Executive Reports 1 (October 15, 1979): 12-16; and Richard Batsavage and John Davie, "China's International Trade and Finance," in Chinese Economy Post-Mao, U.S., Congress, Joint Economic Committee (Washington, D.C.: Government Printing Office, 1978), p. 720.

21. China Business Review, vol. 4 (January-February 1977).

22. Generally, see Financial Times, May 1, 1980; and June 10, 1977; and Wilson, "The Bank of China," p. 106.

23. Melinda Liu, "Hong Kong Banking: China Makes Its Presence Felt," Financial Times, July 19, 1978, p. 28.

24. Financial Times, December 18, 1980, p. 4.

25. Louis Mulkern, "The Financial Aspects of China Trade," in Trade with China, ed. American Management Association (New York: AMA, 1972), p. 20.

26. Economist, May 2, 1981, p. 71.

27. Another quite recent example of the unexplained statistical conflicts is found in a Xinhua News Agency release of February 20, 1981 (quoting the State Statistical Bureau) putting tourists in 1980 at 5.7 million, up 35 percent over 1979. This figure was stated to include business travelers, scientific exchanges, tourists, and other self-financing visitors. On December 18, 1980, the PRC-linked paper, Ta Kung Pao, gave the Government Agency for Travel and Tourism as its source for total tourists in 1979 at 980,000 and expected the 1980 total to reach 1.1 million. These figures differ from those cited in the main text, but the author has tried to allocate the cumulative 1980 figures between compatriots and overseas Chinese. See also conflicting figures in Asian Wall Street Journal Weekly, November 10, 1981, p. 14.

28. Dick Wilson, "The Bank of China," p. 109.

29. See, generally, Far Eastern Economic Review, September 26, 1980; Louis Kraar, "Beijing's Overseas Chinese Connection," Asia 2 (July-August 1979): 4-7, 36-37; and Audrey Donnithorne, China's Economic System (New York: Praeger, 1967), p. 513.

30. Donnithorne, Economic System, p. 513.

31. Ibid.; Wilson, "The Bank of China," p. 109; Mulkern, "Financial Aspects," p. 20; and Dreamer, "Recent Financial Developments," p. 17.

32. Xinhua News Agency release, June 13, 1979.

33. Paul D. Reynolds, "Joint Ventures in China: A Second Look," Company Lawyer, in press, and sources cited therein; and the Law of the People's Republic of China on Joint Ventures Using Chinese and Foreign Investment, reproduced in Paul D. Reynolds, "The Joint Venture Law of the People's Republic of China: Preliminary Observations," International Lawyer 14 (1980): 31-47. See also Martin F. Klingenburg and Joseph Pattison, "Joint Ventures in the People's Republic of China: The New Legal Environment," Virginia Journal of International Law 19 (1979): 807-39.

34. Wall Street Journal, April 23, 1980, p. 19. Two hotel joint ventures, one with the subsidiary of an Ohio company, E-S Pacific Corporation, and another with a company controlled by a Chinese-American and an airline catering firm.

35. Statistics are reported in IMF Survey, April 6, 1981; and Financial Times, June 19, 1981, p. 4. The Xinhua News Agency reported on July 30, 1981, that 131 JVs had opened accounts with the BOC by the end of May. Of these, 105 were based in Guangzhou, 7 in Fuzhou, Fujian, and 19 in Beijing, Shanghai, and other places.

36. On the role of law in China as attracting foreign investment, see Paul D. Reynolds, "The Role of Law in China's Modernization," Poly Law Review 6 (1980): 12-20; and Stanley Lubman, "The Emergence of New Institutions for Trade and Investment in China," in Private Investors Abroad: 1979, ed. Southwestern Legal Foundation (New York: Matthew Bender, 1979), pp. 189-244.

7

FOREIGN SOURCES OF FINANCE

OVERSEAS BONDS AND DEBENTURES

China has given much consideration to selling bonds and debentures in order to raise foreign-source funds, and at least one agency has already done so. The state-owned China International Trust and Investment Corporation (CITIC) offered debt securities through both its Hong Kong and Beijing offices.[1] The first publicized take up was by Eton Corporation, a U.S. company. In early 1980 inquiries were made with Japanese securities companies about the issuance of yen-denominated bonds. While bonds had been issued before, they were limited to purchases by Chinese citizen compatriots (Hong Kong and Macao) or overseas Chinese. A private placement of bonds, the first Chinese bonds denominated in foreign currency since 1949, was announced in March 1981.[2] The issue of ¥10 billion (U.S.$48 million) was to have a maturity of from 15 to 20 years and be handled by the CITIC. The underwriting syndicate, co-led by Nomura Securities, Daiwa Securities, and the Bank of Tokyo, felt that China was not yet eligible to make a public offering under existing Japanese guidelines. It had been hoped that the issue would be placed by the summer of 1981, although terms were delayed when China's cancellation of contracts with Japanese firms in March 1981 caused so much controversy.

Some provinces and large municipalities have been authorized to issue development bonds. The first to act was Fujian Province, which had issued renminbi (RMB)-denominated bonds in the 1950s and 1960s. A plan for industrial-development bonds was announced through Fujian Investment and Enterprise Corporation (also known as Fujian Provincial Investment Enterprise Company or Haufu Company). It was to issue both bearer bonds and order bonds denominated in RMB equivalent to U.S. \$330, \$3,000, and \$33,000; carrying 6 percent interest on an 8-year maturity, 7 percent interest on 10 years, and 8 percent interest on 12 years; which were to be free of all Chinese taxes.[3] The bonds were to be sold through Bank of China (BOC) branches in Fuzhou, the provincial capital, and in Hong Kong at the BOC and other "entrusted banks." The bonds were backed by the Fujian government.[4] The interest rate indicated that the market aimed for was those purchasing for patriotic purposes.[5] The issue of bonds was primarily designed to be bought by wealthy Chinese within China and by overseas Chinese, particularly those in Hong Kong. Other foreigners were not expected to buy them, as the bonds were denominated in Chinese currency. The interest rate was below current international levels in 1980, and unlike most foreign bonds, China's provincial agencies pay interest only once a year. The bonds were not to be listed on any stock exchange, but the BOC agreed to act as agent and was prepared to redeem bonds before maturity. Guangdong Province announced plans in early 1981 to issue bonds through its own Trust and Investment Corporation. The bonds were to be transferable and denominated in foreign currency—units of HK\$2,000 or U.S. \$500. The author was unable to discover an announcement that either bond issue had occurred. The new foreign exchange control regulations may have been used by the General Administration of Exchange Control (GAEC) to stop the provincial governments from proceeding with the issue.

Beijing, like Fujian Province, was considering the issuance of such bonds and consulted with representatives of various Japanese underwriters, such as Daiwa and Nikko, to develop a plan on possible sales to foreigners. The indications were that the debt would be issued in less litigation-prone capital markets than those of the United States or Europe.[6]

Such bonds have an obvious and historic appeal to overseas Chinese and those who buy them for patriotic purposes. However, in international financial markets there are at least two significant problems in any large-scale sale of bonds. First, bond marketing typically requires a very broad market of willing lenders and, in turn, requires the issuer to disclose widespread financial information. For example, the issuance of such bonds in the United States would have to meet the extensive requirements of the Securities and Exchange Commission (SEC).[7] Even though it is unlikely and probably unnecessary to approach heavily regulated markets, such as the United States, some legal questions will cause concern. Will provincial or national law govern? Will China waive sovereign immunity? Will bond terms prevail over changes in exchange controls? An additional legal problem is the outstanding sum of "busted bonds" predating the present Chinese government. About U. S. $70 million worth of such bonds issued during the Boxer Rebellion are outstanding. Many of the bonds issued by various imperial Chinese governments and the Kuomintang are thought to have been destroyed by holders who have long since lost hope of redemption. Of the remainder many are actively traded for collections. Indeed, some of the imperial Chinese bonds are reputed to be worth more than their par value as collector's items. There is no chance whatsoever of the present central government honoring these prerevolutionary debts, and Fujian Province officials have expressly disavowed 1940 loan bonds. Chinese bank officials have stated frequently, in language similar to a recent statement, that "our considered attitude is to renounce them."[8] Nonetheless, at least one bondholder's suit has been brought, with the People's Republic of China named as a defendent (in November 1979 on behalf of nine Alabama holders of prerevolutionary bonds). On November 2, 1981, the U.S. Federal District Court for the Northern District of Alabama issued a default judgment against the People's Republic, holding it responsible for the unpaid principal and interest since 1951 on "Hukuang Railways Sinking Fund Gold Loan" bonds. Should the People's Republic not appeal the judgment within 60 days of the November ruling, its commercial assets within the United States may be subject to seizure.

FOREIGN AID RECEIPTS

China has for many years been a donor of foreign aid to countries in other parts of Asia as well as Africa. Such assistance is considered politically necessary and was continued in the face of its own severe economic needs until quite recently. Just as other economic policies have changed in recent years, China indicated during 1979 that it was now willing to accept foreign aid. Indeed, direct assistance was almost immediately applied for and received from Japan and the United Nations Development Programme (UNDP).

As a significant donor of foreign aid in the past, China's sudden self-transformation into a would-be recipient must be critically examined. A major premise in China's arguments for soft loans and direct grants in aid was a figure that surfaced in 1979 of a per capita income of U.S. $152.[9] At least one commentator and the Central Intelligence Agency (CIA) felt that this figure grossly understated China's achievements, arguing that the figure was based only on output of goods and excluded other sectors, such as services and housing. The CIA had estimated the gross national product (GNP) per capita at U.S. $323 (in 1976 dollars), and the World Bank estimated it at U.S. $390 in 1977. When the World Bank completed its monumental study in June 1981, it produced a revised figure of U.S. $256 per capita, putting China slightly above the average of low-income nations.[10]

Until recently, China would not accept loans or development assistance directly from other governments, but Chinese officials showed an interest in such aid in November 1978, particularly for funds from Japan's Overseas Economic Cooperation Fund (OECF) to build two hydroelectric plants. Requests for funding were also considered for port and railway facilities to be built in connection with a joint Sino-Japanese project to tap undersea oil in the Bohai Gulf. An important factor in overcoming its reluctance to accept foreign aid directly from a national government was the low interest rate (about 3.5 percent) and the long-term repayment provisions of OECF funding.[11]

A formal loan request was made in June 1979 for U.S. $5.2 billion to be used in hydroelectric power plants and railways.[12] The terms requested included an annual interest rate of 2 percent with repayment over 20 to 30 years. Vice-Premier Gu Mu, during his September 1979 visit to Japan, formally asked Prime Minister Ohira for a U.S. $5.54 billion, yen-denominated development loan to finance eight specific projects, including ports. Of the total, U.S. $2.81 billion would presumably be spent in Japan for material and machinery imports. China used former U.S. Vice-President Mondale's promise of a U.S. $2 billion loan from the U.S. Export-Import Bank (Eximbank) as bargaining leverage.

Japan was eager to please China and increase its overall foreign aid program, but the request was too large to be granted. The total of U.S. $5.5 billion was almost five times the sum of all official loans made by Japan in 1978. Japan's overall foreign aid program, including contributions to international financial institutions, was only U.S. $4.86 billion. The request also exceeded Japan's total 1978 exports to China of U.S. $2.05 billion. Japan was concerned over the negative response of its Western allies if easy credit were offered by the Export-Import (Ex-Im) Bank of Japan. Members of the Association of Southeast Asian Nations (ASEAN) were said to be concerned that China's request would diminish the aid available to them. Finally, Japan's already large budget deficit imposed real constraints.

In the end Japan offered substantially less than was asked. During Prime Minister Ohira's December 1979 official visit to China, soft loans worth U.S. $1.5 billion were offered over a six-year period to help China export more coal to Japan. Initially, only U.S. $25 million was granted during early 1980[13] at 3 percent interest with repayment over 30 years with a 10-year grace period. This interest rate was higher than that which China had requested. Although formally linked to port, electric power, and railway development, the loan was informally linked to Japan's hope of importing 7 million tons of coal obtained through related projects. A second installment of U.S. $260 million was made available in December 1980.

The United States had not launched any foreign aid programs for China by early 1981, although during a late 1979 visit Vice-President Mondale had pledged "massive aid on a compensatory basis to develop China's hydro-electric power plants." The aid was to be in the form of loans, but the Chinese felt that the interest rate offered was too high.[14]

If China turns to international aid institutions other than the UNDP, from which it has already received funds, it is likely to seek bilateral aid from countries other than Japan. Certainly, Canadian, French, and West German aid agencies would be sympathetic. In surveying aid the often concessionary loans from export finance agencies must also be considered. Some trade financing can only be described as aid. Several nations have arranged credit tied to purchases within the granting nation. Terms have included very long repayment periods, no interest charges, or low interest charges. In April 1980 Belgium offered China BF300 million interest free for 20 years, but tied it to the purchase of Belgian goods or services.

Through the United Nations Disaster Relief Organization (UNDRO), China has reportedly sought food aid.[15] In March 1981 there were several reports that UNDRO's survey of the food crisis in Hebei and Hubei provinces indicated a need for substantial aid. Informal consultations indicated that most of the 18 or so nations in a position to assist could be willing if China formally asks and makes appropriate credit arrangements. The imports would be large, as several million people are reported to be at risk of malnutrition or near starvation. By June 1981 some individual nations, as well as the European Economic Community, had sent or agreed to send food aid. These initial amounts were small and were probably grants rather than low-interest food credits.

FOREIGN GOVERNMENT-SUPPORTED CREDIT

Most industrial nations have government-supported export credit agencies charged with promoting exports by arranging financial assistance through loan subsidizers, credit insurance, and guarantees. These schemes enable commercial banks to lend without political and commercial risks of nonpayment, which are assumed by the credit agency. The governments of France, Britain, Italy, Japan, Belgium, Australia, Sweden, West Germany, Canada, Argentina, and the United States have negotiated agreements with China providing a wide range of direct credits and subsidized commercial-bank credits designed to stimulate Chinese purchases or promote investment. These nations are bound in principle by a "gentlemen's agreement" periodically revised and renewed; the primary aim is to put a floor under the lowest interest rate.[16] The existence of the agreement has not stopped China from pressing countries, particularly Japan, to lend at rates below the current floor or to avoid other limitations, such as minimum down payments.[17]

Chinese policy toward credits has not been uniform. In early 1980 Yang Bo, vice-chairman of the State Planning Commission, said China could "not use government lines of credit" but instead would "utilize loans, available on the international capital markets."[18] This statement contradicts other policy makers before and since, who had stated a preference for such credit because they have fixed interest rates, frequently low interest, and simpler documentation. In practice, China has used government-supported credits to a much greater degree than commercial-bank financing. In the 1960s and again during the 1970s China has indirectly utilized government-supported credit through supplier credits arranged with the Ex-Im Bank of Japan. The troubled history of those credits is recorded elsewhere.[19] In 1978 the Chinese proposed a change in the relationship and started negotiating directly with the Ex-Im Bank of Japan for buyer's credits. This was agreed upon in August 1978, but only in principle,[20] implementation having been held up over Chinese insistence on dollar credits rather than yen. They believed that yen would continue to appreciate, adding to the repayment burden.

Possibly as a ploy to put negotiating pressure on Japan, China acted on the suggestion of U.K. banks that it arrange its first direct government-backed buyer's credits. Although technically styled a "deposit facility" or "mutual deposit" arrangement, it was a thinly disguised loan directly to the BOC.[21] The London branch of the BOC signed the agreement with seven British banking groups for a total of U.S. $1.2 billion (a sum later greatly enlarged), 85 percent of which was guaranteed by the United Kingdom's Export Credits Guarantee Department (ECGD). The term was for five years and carried an interest rate of 7.25 percent. ECGD assured the banks of a margin over the London interbank offered rate (LIBOR) by subsidizing the difference between that rate and 7.25 percent. No commitment fees, arbitration clauses, termination payments, or management fees were involved, nor were progress payments required. The absence of these provisions was an unusual procedure; for that reason and because of the insights given into China's negotiating technique, the background details merit examination.

While China was carrying on tough negotiations with Japan's Ex-Im Bank in 1978, it was simultaneously acting on the suggestion by the Standard Chartered Bank that use of an ECGD-supported deposit facility would be a way for China to borrow directly without accepting or signing a loan agreement.[22] The ECGD was favorable, because it perceived China as being of the highest credit standing. By October 1978 Standard Chartered's lead had been followed by several banks, including Lloyds Bank International and S. G. Warburg, all of whom were narrowing negotiations toward credits of U.S. $100 million each in the form of ECGD guaranteed deposits. The interest rate was to be around 7.25 percent for the first five years and 7.5 percent thereafter, with terms closely following Japanese bank practices. To facilitate Chinese dislike of lengthy documentation, the ECGD approved the use of a shorter-than-usual guarantee agreement (5 pages instead of 43), and the banks were willing to lend on a deposit basis, hence avoiding the complicated contracts traditional with straight credits. The Chinese also negotiated larger than U.S. $100 million credits with other banks. The ECGD failed to disclose this to earlier creditors, who were annoyed to find that latecomers had negotiated much larger shares; Midland Bank alone produced U.S. $400 million. The ECGD was in some difficulty, because it had set a guarantee ceiling on U.S. $100 million for each of the two original groups. In December 1978 the BOC signed seven separate agreements totaling U.S. $1.2 billion with the following seven bank groups:

Bank	Amount (millions of U.S. dollars)
Midland Bank	400
International Westminster Bank	300
Barclay's Bank	150
Standard Chartered Bank	100
Kleinwort, Benson and the Bank of Scotland	100
S. G. Warburg and Company and Lloyds Bank International	100
Williams and Glyn's Bank and the Royal Bank of Scotland	50

The importance of the agreements, since renewed several times, is that they were the first interbank facilities of their kind negotiated and concluded with the Bank of China and supported by an official credit insurance arrangement.

The Japanese were somewhat shocked and certainly disappointed. As modern China's largest and longest-standing Western trade partner, its bankers had expected to be the first to extend credit. The Ex-Im Bank of Japan was also very concerned that valuable export contracts might be lost to British firms. Another blow was China's acceptance of a U.S.$1 billion dollar-denominated, eight-year line of credit from Italy.[23] This was also negotiated simultaneously during late 1978 but was finalized in January 1979.

Ultimately, this pressure succeeded in getting the Ex-Im Bank of Japan to move forward the implementation of a not-yet-finalized scheme to enable it to meet China's demands for dollar financing at rates lower than those it had already obtained. The agreement secured a U.S.$2 billion (approximately) 15-year line of credit at 6.25 percent a year. This rate was 1 percent below the minimum interest rate then established by the OECD "gentlemen's agreement" on export credits, and pressure to better the ECGD's terms caused the Ex-Im Bank of Japan to put itself in the awkward position of justifying the breach. Japan argued that the agreement was inapplicable, as it was for development purposes and not exports, and in any event, was not limited to Japanese exports.[24] U.S. and European reaction was negative. The United States considered the loan to break the spirit, if not the letter, of the agreement and caustically commented on Japan's "fairly creative and unique definition of the loan."[25]

TABLE 10

Government Credit Agreements with China, as of December 31, 1980

Country	Date	Amount (millions of U.S. dollars)	Terms	Notes
United Kingdom	12/78	1,200	Ten years; 7.25 percent for first five years; 7.5 percent thereafter	Bank consortium; guaranteed and interest subsidized by ECGD
	3/79	3,800	Six years; same as 12/78	Government-to-government credit agreement guaranteeing ECGD would provide $5 billion total-supported credit, including agreed amount from 12/78
Australia[a]	4/79	56 ($A50 million)	Not available; 7.25 percent	Export Finance and Insurance Corporation for purchase of Australian products
	6/79	23	Five years; same as 4/79	Same as 4/79; for eight hotels
France	5/79	7,000[b] (Fr30 billion)	Same as U.K. consortium of 12/78	Consortium of 18 banks; guaranteed by COFACE; for purchase of French goods and services
Italy	5/79	1,000	Repayment over eight and one-half years; 7.25 percent	Consortium of financial institutions put together at government behest; for purchase of Italian products

(continued)

TABLE 10 (continued)

Country	Date	Amount (millions of U.S. dollars)	Terms	Notes
Japan	5/79	2,000[b]	Ten years plus five-year option; 6.5 percent	Ex-Im Bank of Japan for resource development of OECF aid; $225 million in 1979; $250 million in 1980; $1,156 billion from 1981 to 1986
	5/79	1,625[b]	3.5 percent	
Sweden	5/79	350[b]	Not available	Swedish Export Credit Corporation
Argentina	6/79	300	Not available	Not available; purchases of Argentinian goods
Canada[c]	8/79	1,720[b]	Five years; 7.25 percent	Export Development Corporation; for purchase of Canadian goods and services
Federal Republic of Germany	10/79	1,100[b]	Not available	Not available
Belgium	11/79	173[b]	20 years; interest free	Tied to purchase of Belgian goods and services

[a]The Far Eastern Economic Review (see below) gives the total as U.S.$45 million.

[b]Loans are denominated in local currency, and their dollar value may change from time to time.

[c]The Far Eastern Economic Review (see below) gives total as U.S.$2,311. China Business Consultants give total as U.S.$2 billion, signed May 1979.

Sources: China Business Review, January-February 1980, p. 57; Far Eastern Economic Review, September 21, 1979, p. 45; and unpublished survey by China Business Consultants, 1979.

By March 1980, less than a year after changing policy, China had arranged loans or lines of credit totaling U. S. $31 billion, of which fully U. S. $20 billion was underwritten by governments (see Table 10). By early 1981 very little of these credits had been drawn down.[26] One reason for this, and another advantage of such government credits, is that China has usually been able to avoid management and commitment fees, thus depriving the financings of a built-in incentive to use the credits. The only reported exception, though unconfirmed, is the French medium-term credit of U. S. $7 billion in francs. This was said to be unusual in that it included management and commitment fees and required an early and substantial drawing.[27] Without these up front and carrying costs in most of its agreements, China had nothing to lose while, at the same time, giving its financial planners additional flexibility. With low-interest, fixed-rate, medium-term financing sewed up, the Chinese had increased their bargaining leverage in negotiating longer-term credits elsewhere. It had done this at little cost; through highly favorable terms; at low, fixed interest rates; and through encouraging competition among exporting governments. In late 1981 nations that were party to the "gentlemen's agreement" agreed to a substantial increase in the floor rates and agreed to work toward periodic revisions aimed at keeping the floor rates in line with other market rates. The immediate effect on China's existing lines of credit is unclear, but future credit agreements will be more costly until worldwide interest rates drop from their current highs.

INTERNATIONAL FINANCIAL ORGANIZATIONS

China has now joined, become actively involved in, and sought loans from several different international financial organizations (IFOs) and programs. Some of the programs, such as UNDP and UNDRO have already been cited. This section examines the recent evolution of China's role in the other organizations. That involvement is sufficiently complex that the government has established a steering group to coordinate dealing with IFOs. It comprises members from the Finance Ministry, State Planning Commission, Capital Construction Commission, and the banks.

The International Monetary Fund

It was natural for China, a developing nation, to consider taking advantage of the many international financial institutions established to assist countries with their long-term development or short-term balance-of-payments difficulties. After China's Cultural Revolution ended, and again after the People's Republic displaced Taiwan in China's seat at the United Nations, considerable speculation arose around the prospects for the People's Republic becoming a full member of the International Monetary Fund (IMF). In 1946 China had become an original founder of the IMF, so the issue was technically one of successor governments, rather than one of new membership. With a capital subscription of U.S. $550 million, 15 percent paid in the form of gold, China was the fifth largest member by quota size.

Speculation over new membership or displacement of Taiwanese control of China's seat was particularly strong in 1978 and 1979. Fueled by questions and hints directed at Western businessmen, anticipation rose until China contacted the IMF in early 1980. In response to an invitation, the IMF sent a mission to Beijing in late March 1980. At the time these technical-level talks were described as "exploratory."[28] Four weeks later the IMF and the International Bank for Reconstruction and Development (World Bank) suddenly announced that the People's Republic of China had been substituted for Taiwan as a member of these organizations.[29]

The seemingly quick change was the result of long and complex negotiations with the IMF, China, and the U.S. Congress.[30] In the early 1970s China had insisted that Taiwan (the Republic of China) must first be expelled from the IMF and World Bank before China would participate. In 1979 and 1980 this position was moderated on several occasions. Taiwan was not expelled in 1980, but the representation of China was changed.

The difficult question of China's quota was partially resolved. As stated, Taiwan had paid in 15 percent of its original quota in gold, 10 percent in foreign exchange, and 75 percent in national currency. Many nations paid part of their quota in gold. In 1976 the IMF decided to sell part of its gold holding and to allow member countries to buy some of it at Special Drawing Right (SDR) 32 per ounce. Because of the uncertainty of the PRC's intentions, China's (Taiwan's) distribution was not yet made in early 1980. When the PRC made clear its intention to assume IMF membership, negotiations opened over the gold. There was strong opposition in some quarters to the PRC obtaining this gold. In the end the IMF sold to the Republic of China (Taiwan) 470.7 million ounces of gold at SDR 32 per ounce, and the Republic of China paid the IMF SDR 107.6 million to replenish the foreign exchange tranche of China's seat, which was taken over by the PRC. At that time China's quota remained at SDR 550 million, the issue of a new increased quota being put off pending further economic studies.

When China originally became an IMF member in 1946, its capital quota was quite low for a nation its size because of the low level of development. Membership of the government of the People's Republic made it necessary for a new capital quota to be set.[31] China requested this during an IMF team visit in July 1980, and in September its quota was raised to SDR 1.2 billion, equivalent at that time to U.S.$1,580 million. As of December 1980 the quota of all IMF members who consented to the increase was raised by 50 percent. China's quota in 1981, therefore, stood at SDR 1.8 billion (about U.S.$2.3 billion). The quota is paid 75 percent in RMB and 25 percent in hard currencies. This figure must be seen in light of Japan's quota of U.S.$3.2 billion and India's quota of U.S.$2.2 billion. The immediate direct effect was to increase China's voting power and to increase its access to IMF resources. This can be done through a variety of lending schemes available to members, particularly developing-nation members. While access to IMF resources is quasi-automatic under certain schemes, it is subject to gradually increasing restrictive terms under others. These restrictions, referred to as conditionality, are normally set out in a "standby arrangement"[32] between the IMF and the member country, whereby the member takes upon itself to implement certain policy measures to promote balance-of-payments equilibrium. China's quota in other international bodies will also be tied to a proportion of the IMF quota. An indirect effect of membership and borrowing is often an enhanced ability to borrow funds from private banks, something China has had no difficulty with thus far.

The first IMF borrowing for China was requested in early 1981 after a late 1980 IMF staff visit.[33] The borrowing was agreed by March 1981, and a standby loan of SDR 450 million (about U.S.$540 million) in support of "a stabilization programme" was made available under the first credit tranche of China's quota.[34] The standby arrangement was for 12 months. At about the same time China drew down its reserve position at the IMF by SDR 300 million and received a Trust Fund Loan amounting to SDR 309 million.[35] Trust Fund Loans (a special account containing proceeds of IMF gold sales) are given at 0.5 percent interest and are repayable in six semiannual installments beginning after the sixth year (see Table 11).

TABLE 11

Credits Supplied by International Organizations to China

Organization	Date	Amount (millions)	Notes
United Nations Development Programme	1979	Not available	Consultant and planning fees
International Monetary Fund	3/81	SDR 450	About U.S. $450 million; 12-month standby credit in support of "stabilization"
	3/81	SDR 300	Withdrawal of reserves
	3/81	SDR 309	Trust fund loan at 0.5 percent annual interest; repayable in six semiannual installments after six-year grace period
International Fund for Agricultural Development	5/81	U.S. $35	Not available
International Development Agency and World Bank	6/81	U.S. $200	One-half from each at 9.6 percent interest from the World Bank and nearly interest-free terms from IDA for education projects
United Nations Disaster Relief Organization		Not available	Aid package for famine relief not finalized by June 1981

Sources: Various issues of Asian Wall Street Journal.

China's full membership in the International Monetary Fund has several additional important implications, most stemming from the requirements of membership. Key requirements under Article 8 of the Fund Agreement include a provision of detailed information on official foreign exchange holdings; gold production figures; total exports and imports in terms of local-currency values; trade figures broken down by country of destination and origin; information on balance of payments, including capital flows and invisibles; national income; price indexes; and foreign debt. In addition to this information, China must also allow a comprehensive IMF survey of its economy by both the IMF and World Bank staff; this has already been completed. It must also agree to set the value of RMB at an exchange rate that will not damage competitive currencies. Finally, China must be willing to consult annually with the staff of the IMF and, subsequently, the staff of the World Bank to discuss the state of its economy and must meet any conditions imposed by the IMF on borrowings. China may follow Romania's lead and ask the IMF to keep financial information confidential, although this would be unusual.

That the government of China will have difficulty in supplying some of the required information is to be expected. China's response has been that some of the required information has simply not been available in the past because of an inability to accurately gather certain information at the present time. The problem of exaggeration by local officials in their reports is just one additional hurdle to overcome. Another is recent conflicts in official and semiofficial statistical reports. Certainly, early consultations with the IMF staff will lead to measures designed to overcome the defects in information-gathering techniques.

The World Bank

With China's membership in the IMF, a major hurdle to World Bank membership was cleared; a nation cannot become a member of the World Bank and have access to its low-cost funds without first being a member of the IMF. Several nations, like India and Indonesia, were concerned that their share of World Bank funds would be greatly reduced by the entry of a large new borrower. The World Bank's staff itself expressed doubt about its ability to quickly study China, obtain accurate statistics, and then formulate a lending policy. A significant lag between membership and actual loans was anticipated.

Although the lobby for Taiwan's membership in the World Bank was stronger than its lobby was within the IMF, the change in membership at the World Bank was simultaneous with that at the IMF.[36] China's willingness to join both the IMF and the World Bank had been signaled by Vice-Premier Gu Mu on September 28, 1979, when he said that China was "ready to accede to the IMF, the World Bank, and the United Nations Development Program as well as accept loans from the World Bank." The minister of finance was appointed China's governor to the IMF and World Bank group in June 1980.[37]

Under the urging of outgoing President Robert McNamara, the World Bank acted speedily to approve its first loan to China within 13 months of its admission. The IDA and the bank provided U.S.$100 million each to finance a variety of education projects at 44 institutions to assist in massive increases in undergraduate and postgraduate enrollment. Two other loans are being processed in late 1981. Port projects in these provinces might be lent U.S.$200 million and irrigation projects, another U.S.$80 million to U.S.$100 million.

As part of the first loan's terms, China was asked to establish standard procedures for awarding contracts in international bidding —routine in World Bank loans. Any component purchase or project over U.S.$100,000 within the overall plan must be reviewed by the bank's staff. Loan negotiations were protracted over the ratio of nearly interest-free IDA money to 10 percent World Bank funds. The bank estimated that China could afford a ratio of one part IDA funds to three parts World Bank funds. The Chinese view that only a 50:50 ratio was affordable won out. However, the initial lending program of U.S.$800 million was delayed, and only the U.S.$200 million education project was approved, since the bank accepted that education required financing at lower-than-normal interest rates.

Other International Financial Organizations

China is probably most interested in borrowing from the International Development Agency (IDA), which is the concessionary lending arm of the World Bank. The IDA lends to countries with per capita GNPs of no more than U.S.$600. The general view in 1980 was that China appeared to qualify, but strong doubts were expressed about the accuracy of preliminary GNP statistics. However, the

World Bank completed the first full-length study in June 1981 and arrived at a per capita sum of U. S. $256, about the same as Pakistan or Tanzania.[38] The IDA itself is regularly and quickly run down in funding, having been replenished recently for the sixth time. The outlook for the seventh replenishment was grim in late 1981. At present some 40 percent of IDA loans are pledged to India; any major financing for China will require either a further replenishment or reduction in India's proportion of funds, something with which that country has already expressed concern.[39]

The International Fund for Agricultural Development made a loan to China in mid-1981. The loan was for U. S. $35 million and at a low interest rate. The purpose was to support pasture development. This fund is also exhausted, but efforts to replenish it may be complete by 1982.

At the time of writing, China had not yet joined the Asian Development Bank (ADB) but had frequently indicated its desire to do so. When it does join, China will be the largest member and, potentially, the largest borrower. The institutional, financial, and political changes for the ADB, as well as for the World Bank and the IMF, could be enormous. Certainly, the balance of power within these international financial institutions will be altered. This comes at a time when the importance of these institutions has dramatically increased through their role in assisting developing nations to cope with the effects of oil price rises.

NOTES

1. See the Wall Street Journal, December 13, 1979, p. 33, col. 4, for background information.

2. Financial Times, March 5, 1981, p. 40, col. 2; and Japan Economic Journal, October 13, 1981, p. 1.

3. The most detail is found in an interview with Fujian's deputy governor, Zhany Yi, in Far Eastern Economic Review, January 18, 1980, pp. 51-52. Also see James Stepanek, "Fujian Bonds?" China Business Review 7 (March-April 1980): 54; Xinhua News Agency release, January 29, 1980; and the Wall Street Journal, January 30, 1980, p. 19, col. 2.

4. Far Eastern Economic Review, January 18, 1980, pp. 51-52; but China Business Review 7 (March-April 1980): 54, reported that the bonds could not be backed by the government.

5. "Chinese Bonds: Fujian Puts Out a Feeler," Economist, February 2, 1980, p. 86.

6. Ibid.; Financial Times, January 29, 1980; and Japan Economic Journal, October 13, 1981, p. 1.

7. Wall Street Journal, January 29, 1980, p. 5, col. 4.

8. Dick Wilson, "How Banks Work in China," Banker 130 (January 1980): 22; and Economist, February 2, 1980, p. 86.

9. Further details can be found in Economist, October 6, 1979, p. 84.

10. Reported in ibid., June 20, 1981, pp. 34-35.

11. Financial Times World Business Weekly, November 13, 1978, p. 28; Far Eastern Economic Review, February 2, 1979, p. 42; and U.S., Congress, Committee on International Relations, A New Realism: Factfinding Mission to the People's Republic of China, July 3-13, 1978 (Washington, D.C.: Government Printing Office, 1978), pp. 78-79.

12. See, generally, the Wall Street Journal, August 21, 1979, p. 24, col. 4; September 10, 1979, p. 18, col. 1; and Asian Wall Street Journal Weekly, October 8, 1979, p. 4.

13. Tracy Dahlby, "A Cautious Helping Hand," Far Eastern Economic Review, December 14, 1979, p. 100; Wall Street Journal, December 10, 1979, p. 14, col. 2; and April 7, 1980, p. 26, col. 5. Further details are available in Tracy Dahlby, "Japan's China Extravaganza," Far Eastern Economic Review, November 16, 1979, pp. 56-58; and Economist, December 8, 1979, pp. 71-72.

14. Bureau of National Affairs, International Trade Reporter, no. 271 (August 28, 1979), p. C-1; and Wilson, "How Banks Work," p. 22.

15. John Wyles, "China Turns to U.N. in Food Crisis," Financial Times, March 9, 1981, p. 22, col. 1. See also David Bonavia, "Food: A Nightmare Shortfall," Far Eastern Economic Review, May 15, 1981, p. 96.

16. The OECD Arrangement on Guidelines for Officially Supported Credits (OECD Document no. TC/CONSENSUS/78.4) as periodically revised is an informal arrangement, which imposes no sanctions but is designed to prevent unfair international competition through low-interest credit subsidization of exports, long a controversial issue in international trade. The guideline prohibitions are not binding but do require a lending country to notify other members when it desires to deviate from guidelines.

17. Richard Batsavage and John Davie, "China's International Trade and Finance," in Chinese Economy Post-Mao, U.S., Congress, Joint Economic Committee (Washington, D.C.: Government Printing Office, 1978), p. 732; and "A New Capitalist Role for the People's Bank," Business Week, September 1978, p. 704.

18. Asian Wall Street Journal Weekly, February 8, 1980, p. 13, col. 3.

19. Dan Henderson and Tasuku Matsuo, "Trade with Japan," in Law and Politics in China's Foreign Trade, ed. Victor Li (Berkeley and Los Angeles: University of California Press, 1977), pp. 39-40, 66-67; Alistair Wrightman, "How Japan Finances Trade with China," U.S.-China Business Review 2 (March-April 1975): 30-33; and Gene T. Hsiao, The Foreign Trade of China: Policy, Law, and Practice (Berkeley and Los Angeles: University of California Press, 1977), p. 58.

20. New York Times, August 18, 1978, p. 9, col. 4; and Financial Times, August 29, 1978.

21. Financial Times World Business Weekly, December 4, 1978, pp. 25-26; New York Times, December 2, 1978, p. 7, col. 2; and Far Eastern Economic Review, January 19, 1979, p. 80.

22. Financial Times, December 1, 1978; and Yorkshire Post, December 6, 1978.

23. Financial Times World Business Weekly, November 6, 1978, p. 22.

24. "Chinese Borrowing on the International Capital Markets," International Currency Review 11 (1979): 47-49.

25. Bureau of National Affairs, International Trade Reporter, no. 270 (October 2, 1979), p. C-1; and (March 11, 1980), p. C-5.

26. In order to encourage use of the U.K. credit facility, England's ECGD has twice reduced the minimum contract value eligible for funding from £5 million to £1 million to less than £1 million.

27. "Chinese Borrowing on the International Capital Markets," p. 49.

28. Wall Street Journal, April 17, 1980, p. 12, col. 3.

29. IMF Survey, 1980, p. 113.

30. James Stepanek, "China, the IMF, and the World Bank," China Business Review 7 (January-February 1980): 56; Dinah Lee, "China Joins the Money Club," South, August 1980, pp. 52-53; and Anthony Rowley, "Changing the Power Balance," Far Eastern Economic Review, April 25, 1980, p. 85.

31. For a background on calculations and predictions of the quota, see Stepanek, "China, the IMF"; and Economist, October 6, 1979, p. 74. Changes in the quotas and their calculations have occurred since those articles were written.

32. For further details, see Joseph Gold, Conditionality (Washington, D.C.: International Monetary Fund, 1980), or the summary in David L. Denny, "International Finance in the People's Republic of China," in China: A Reassessment of the Economy, U.S., Congress, Joint Economic Committee (Washington, D.C.: Government Printing Office, 1975), p. 674.

33. Financial Times, February 14, 1981, p. 26, col. 2.

34. Times (London), March 3, 1981, p. 15, col. 8.

35. Letter from Luc DeWolf of the International Monetary Fund, May 5, 1981.

36. Wall Street Journal, April 25, 1980, p. 17, col. 2.

37. Bureau of National Affairs, International Trade Reporter, no. 276 (October 2, 1979), p. C-1.

38. Ibid.; and Wall Street Journal, April 25, 1980, p. 17, col. 2. China submitted to the World Bank in 1980 a per capita income figure of U.S.$230, whereas the bank's staff had previously estimated U.S.$466. Other figures, such as those of the Central Intelligence Agency, had been much higher but were based on a methodology not designed for international comparison. The doubts and dilemmas caused by these conflicting figures are dealt with in the section on foreign aid in Chapter 6.

39. Lee, "China Joins the Money Club," p. 53. See also "India May Top Asian Bank," American Banker, October 15, 1981, p. 18, indicating that India appears likely to increase its borrowings from the Asian Development Bank as a fallback against China draining off World Bank funds.

8

COMMERCIAL BANK FINANCING

INITIAL BORROWINGS

Beginning in March 1979 many commercial bank loans were arranged with banks from several countries lending singly or through a syndicate. These were all direct loans and described as such. By June 1979, after just three months, the total reached U. S. $3.4 billion. Although China had been borrowing for many years on a short- to medium-term basis through a variety of indirect devices, the possibilities of large, direct commercial credits caused the most excitement within the international banking community. These banks will continue to be cash rich and short of first-quality borrowers for many years to come.

When it became widely known that China was considering direct commercial borrowing, speculation focused on a likely interest rate of 1 percent above the London interbank offered rate (LIBOR) with total borrowings of U.S.$12 billion. Of that total, commercial banks might lend U.S.$3 billion to U.S.$4 billion in 1979-81. But within a year China had actually been able to line up almost U.S.$30 billion—over U.S.$11 billion commercially—and at interest rates as low as 0.25 percent above LIBOR (see Tables 10, 11, and 12). The successful steps and methods used obviously merit detailed examination.

TABLE 12

Publicized Commercial Bank (Buyer's) Credits

Lender	Date	Amount (millions of U.S. dollars)	Interest[a]	Notes
Lloyds Bank International	March 1979	100	0.5	Five-year loan to the BOC not linked to any specific project
Midland & International Banks (plus Austrian, British, and Canadian banks)	March 1979	175	0.5	Five-year loan to the BOC not linked to any specific project
National Westminster	March 1979	100	0.5	Five-year loan to the BOC not linked to any specific project
Standard Chartered	March 1979	100	0.5	Five-year loan to the BOC not linked to any specific project
Midland	March 1979	100	0.5	Five-year loan to the BOC not linked to any specific project
Union des Banques Arabes et Françaises (UBAF) led syndicate of Arab bank members of UBAF	February 1980	300	0.5	Eurodollar three-and-one-half year bullet loan to the BOC not tied to contracts; originally U.S.$500 million, but finalized at U.S.$300
Canadian Imperial Bank of Commerce	April 1979	100	Not available	Five-year loan to the BOC not tied to contracts
Chase Manhattan Bank	April 1979	30	Not available	Term not available: tied to design costs of Beijing trade center; loan subsequently canceled.
Bank of Chile	April 1979	10	Not available	Not available; tied to trade with Chile
Chase Manhattan Bank	May 1979	200	Not available	For construction costs of the Beijing trade center; subsequently canceled, revived, and recanceled
Bank of Tokyo led 22-bank syndicate	February 1979[b]	2,000	0.5	Eurodollar four-and-one-half year loan to the BOC for export financing
Bank of Tokyo led 31-bank syndicate	May 1979[b]	6,000	0.25	Six-month export refinancing

First National Bank of Chicago	May 1979	8	Not available	Short-term ship financing with provision for immediate drawdown by Fujian Provincial Investment Corporation; guaranteed by the BOC
Norddeutsche Landesbank-Giro Zentrale (through two affiliates)	August 1979	50	0.5[c]	Five years export credit
Bayerische Vereinsbank of Munich	August 1979	100	Not available	Eurodollar two-year loan to be drawn down within six months
First City National Bank of Houston	November 1979	10	Not available	Unnamed borrower in Fujian Province
First National Bank of Chicago	October 1979	20	Not available	Fujian Province
Hong Kong-Shanghai	March 1980	30	Not available	For construction of a hotel in Nanjing with a two-year grace period; unconfirmed
Nordic Bank, Limited, led syndicate	March 1981	72	Not available	To Great Wall Hotel, joint venture of Beijing; lenders included the BOC (London branch)
Canadian Imperial Bank of Canada	June 1981	42	Not available	To the Shin Ho Ch'eng Development Company of Hong Kong to construct China (Guangzhou) Hotel in Guangdong
First National Bank of Chicago	November 1981	3.7	Not available	Export credit facility to the BOC for China Machine Building International and National Electric Equipment Corporation; guaranteed by Eximbank

[a]Percent over LIBOR unless stated otherwise.
[b]The package of Japanese bank and Ex-Im Bank of Japan credits were "agreed" some months before being finally signed.
[c]Estimate.

Note: Interest rates on the above loans vary according to the length of maturity and prevailing rates while the loans are outstanding. The general pattern is 0.5 percent over LIBOR. LIBOR stood at 12.3 in December 1978 and 14.4 in December 1979 (for six-months credit), during which time most of the above were agreed. LIBOR averaged 17 percent during 1981. A BOC official has mentioned a loan from a Norwegian lender, but no details are available to the author.

Sources: Reports in the New York Times, the Times (London), the Financial Times, the Wall Street Journal, the Asian Wall Street Journal Weekly, various issues; and the China Business Review, January-February 1980, p. 57.

The first commercial bank loan by a Western bank was announced in March 1979. The Bank of China (BOC) borrowed U.S.$175 million for five years from Midland and International Bank Limited, which was acting with other British, Australian, and Canadian banks.[1] The general trade credit was handled as a single bank facility, rather than a formal syndicated credit. At about the same time four other banks arranged separate but similar loans. (see Table 12). These were the first commercial loans, but most attention was focused on the yet-to-be-arranged first large Eurodollar loan by a syndicate to banks.

LOAN NEGOTIATIONS

After Japan and China signed a long-term trade agreement in February 1978, negotiations started with Japanese banks and the Ex-Export-Import (Ex-Im) Bank of Japan for a package of suppliers' credits and later buyer's credits. With the widespread belief that China was about to change its policy on loans, 75 bank delegations visited China in the 12-month period to May 1979.[2] Perceiving its attractiveness and high credit rating in the eyes of the international community, China also saw the potential to use the community's competitiveness. In the words of Diether Hoffman, cochair of Bank für Gemeinwirtshaft of West Germany, "They know they are considered a number one potential borrower and will receive appropriate terms. They will do everything possible to make use of competition among lending banks."[3] By late 1978, therefore, Japan's bankers must have felt pressure to come to terms. The Ex-Im Bank of Japan offered the equivalent of U.S.$1 billion for oil and gas development in a five-year, yen-denominated loan, and the Bank of Tokyo tentatively lined up in a syndicate to lend U.S.$2 billion by December 1978.[4] By February 4, 1979, it felt able to announce a "basic agreement."[5] The wording is important, because reported "agreements" in Chinese trade have often turned out to be premature or, in reality, only agreements to negotiate, subject to further negotiation, or only memoranda of understanding. In fact, the final package of agreements had been (and was to remain) stalled over two issues for several months. China desired dollar financing, because it was quite confident that the dollar would decline or at least not appreciate, while it feared the yen would continue to appreciate. Furthermore, it sought lower interest rates than were being offered.

On February 15, 1979, agreement on the Ex-Im Bank of Japan's subsidized credit for U.S.$2 billion was announced, with repayment to be made in crude oil if oil was found in the Bohai Gulf; otherwise repayment was to be in cash.[6] Again, "details were to be worked out." By March a total of 22 Japanese banks had joined negotiations, and the figures had become U.S.$2 billion denominated in dollars for five years at 0.625 percent over LIBOR, combined with a revolving (short-term) credit of U.S.$6 billion at 0.375 percent over LIBOR. Later in March it was "agreed" to extend the term for eight years instead of five. Outside observers sensed things were not going smoothly. The Economist said, "Tokyo likes to give the impression that these deals . . . are now virtually in the bag. But it is showing some signs of nerves."[7] The Wall Street Journal carefully referred to a "tentative agreement."[8]

As prolonged negotiation seemed to be leading toward higher interest rates, and while the Japanese were confident of concluding the first agreement, the entire banking community was stunned at the announcement that China had placed its first syndicated loan through the Arab bank shareholders/members of Union des Banques Arabes et Françaises (UBAF).[9] UBAF agreed to the exceptionally low interest rate of 0.5 percent over LIBOR. China succeeded in gaining agreement, thereby establishing the precedent that it was a first-class credit risk entitled to borrow at below what Japan had offered. Indeed, because the UBAF loan was untied, it was felt that China could properly argue for future export-related loans to carry even lower interest rates, since banks are more sure of repayment, and their own corporate customers directly profit. In fact, this is exactly what happened.

The UBAF loan had not been signed and was not signed for almost another year. Yet, China's negotiators proved their deftness at extracting the best terms possible by using the leverage provided by the UBAF loan to win even more favorable terms from the disquieted Japanese.[10] A month later Japanese bankers announced an agreement, which included a development loan stretched out over ten years, a syndicated credit with interest pared down from 0.625 to 0.5 percent (matching UBAF), and short-term credit at the wafer-thin margin of 0.25 percent over LIBOR, down from 0.375 percent.[11] The latter was the lowest margin then publicly announced, and there was considerable speculation that some methods to raise the effective rate would be taken by the banks involved.[12] The final agreements were to be signed that week. Even at that stage China was not finished trying to obtain the best terms possible.

This demonstrates a negotiating technique often used by Chinese bankers and traders. Frequently, the Chinese negotiator only agrees to a preliminary agreement or memorandum of understanding. Such an agreement whets the appetite of foreign banks (flush with excess liquidity). The Chinese negotiator then stretches out negotiations over the "final details." It was not surprising, therefore, that the Bank of Tokyo announcement in May 1979 was cautiously worded. Reports noted that the "basic loan agreement(s) . . . were general agreements . . . in that they are frameworks for the final agreements still to be signed. Not all the details have been signed" (emphasis added).[13] Those details must have included issues such as documentation, economic data, arbitration, management and commitment fees, and sovereign immunity, all of which had been settled unusually and to China's satisfaction in the UBAF agreement. A similar process occurred with Chase Manhattan Bank's loan of U.S.$30 million in April 1979, which subsequently turned into a not-to-be-finalized framework agreement.

LOAN PRACTICES: DOCUMENTATION, FEES, TERMS, AND DRAWINGS

The Arab bankers in the UBAF group had been eager to secure a large, syndicated credit agreement and in February 1979 had offered U.S.$1 billion for ten years.[14] In response to China's concern over the length of maturity, its desire to limit lenders to Arab banks, and its concern to keep execution simple, a smaller, short-term agreement was proposed and agreed upon. However, in the detailed negotiations that followed, China extracted several concessions that proved to be valuable precedents. In the face of Chinese objections to providing extensive economic data, customary in large, syndicated credits to developing nations, UBAF agreed to waive the normal "placing memorandum" and substitute a single sheet merely outlining the terms.[15] This was not totally novel, as it is understood that the USSR had also gained this privilege.

It is common, if not normal, for governments and their agencies to waive sovereign immunity and expressly submit to the jurisdiction of foreign courts to hear claims arising from their loans. Understandably, governments resist giving this waiver whenever possible. China successfully objected to giving such a waiver, and the UBAF agreement called for dispute settlement in China. Most unusual of all, it substituted arbitration for judicial proceedings.

UBAF also agreed to forgo its customary management fee, a flat fee paid by the lender for arrangement of the loan. Most significantly, no commitment fee was charged; a commitment fee is calculated as a percentage payment on all funds committed to the loan but not yet drawn. The combined effect was that the BOC could sign the loan without incurring any initial direct cost and suffer no further costs if it decided not to draw funds.[16]

This is precisely what has happened. Reports from a wide number of sources confirm that both the UBAF and the Bank of Tokyo syndicated credits, as well as most single-bank commercial credits, have remained largely or entirely unused through early 1981. Some bankers reportedly felt that China had at least a good faith obligation to act on existing lines of credit and has, therefore, breached that obligation by arranging but not utilizing these loans. However, most commercial credit is offered to China at floating rates, which since 1979 have generally been above 15 percent; government-supported credits, on the other hand, are available at 7.25 percent. In the case of Japan, China has not used the syndicated credits at all and, despite its stated preference for dollars over yen, has used the especially low-interest yen, Ex-Im Bank of Japan credit despite some appreciation of the yen against the dollar in early 1980.[17] The large-scale cancellations of contracts with Japanese companies in latc 1980 and carly 1981 madc it appear virtually certain China would not use the Eurodollar credits, which had been informally earmarked for the projects canceled by economic planners. Chinese bankers were said to be interested in raising new united low-interest loans to replace the tied Ex-Im Bank of Japan credits. But Japanese bankers reacted negatively, being disinclined to negotiate until the legal issues of canceled contracts were cleared up. Several contracts have been reconfirmed or rescheduled, and thus, it is unclear which, if any, will finally be canceled. Whatever happens, Japan's bankers will be slow to once again commit themselves and tie down funds without earning any significant fee income. New private-bank commercial loans have been offered as part of the Japanese government's package to solve the suspended contract problem. Agreement on the package was reached on December 16, 1981.

Some other borrowing practices are noteworthy. China has spread its borrowing around. It has not concentrated on one country, currency, bank, or group of banks. Borrowing sources have also been diversified, with commercial creditors competing with aid donors, official credit agencies, private investors, and international financial institutions. The main objective of China's financiers has been to maintain flexibility in sources and avoid excessive dependence on any one source or currency. Policy on debt limits has also been flexible and pragmatic, with no fixed ratios regarding sources or overall totals. One policy statement has recognized that a 22 percent to 25 percent debt-to-export ratio was "the safety limit," and that China has self-imposed limits of not exceeding 15 percent to 20 percent of exports through 1990.[18] On this basis the policy makers anticipated a maximum borrowing of U.S. $50 billion, very little of which was to be commercial bank loans.

For obvious political reasons it has not been possible for China to expressly include loan-repayment plans in the national budget until quite recently. This has been done only since 1980, when repayments of principle and interest were allocated RMB 2.17 billion (U.S.$1.5 billion approximately), leaving total foreign debt outstanding at the end of fiscal 1980 at U.S.$3.4 billion.[19] The officially published 1979 actual budget and 1980 interim budget list total foreign borrowing of RMB 13.4 billion (U.S.$8.9 billion approximately).

There has been concern over questions of legal borrowing authority. The novelty of borrowing abroad, combined with the widespread absence of economic laws, has made it difficult to determine whether prospective borrowers other than the BOC have authority (for example, provincial governments, foreign trade corporations, and regional investment corporations). The BOC itself maintains an authorized signature list, which its correspondents can use to check the authority of BOC officers. The issue is important and not moot. A vice-minister of the petroleum industry is said to have made secret and unauthorized approaches while in Brussels to Belgian banks seeking large loans.[20] A China radio editorial describing the incident urged severe punishment. The national government also perceived and confirmed the problem's existence when issuing the new Exchange Control Regulations;[21] Article 5 subjects all national and provincial enterprises and government establishments to the controls. Articles 6 and 8 require these bodies to have General Administration of Exchange Control (GAEC) approval to obtain foreign exchange or borrow abroad. Section 6 prohibits borrowing through "state organs stationed abroad," a suggestion that this unauthorized activity has been a problem. The regulations now put foreign banks on notice that borrowers must show an annual borrowing plan approved by the GAEC and State Council, as well as their approval of the specific loan contemplated. Foreign banks are also on notice that loan proceeds must be deposited with the BOC, which is charged with supervising onward payments to the borrower.

Finally the BOC's involvement in foreign bank loans ranges from most often being the immediate borrower to being a colender (twice in 1980). The BOC frequently grants a guarantee of full repayment, but on some occasions it has merely witnessed or acknowledged the agreement.[22] Doubts expressed over its legal authority to issue guarantees have not been quashed, because the new Articles of Association do not expressly give the bank this power (see Appendix A).

PROSPECTS

Despite these problems and the low levels of profits for banks lending to China, there are substantial reasons to anticipate that China will borrow more and can do so without significant difficulties. First, the international banking community is notoriously competitive. China knows how to turn that competitiveness to its advantage. Its bargaining skills, use of leverage, and use of competitiveness among lenders has been extraordinary. When a borrower becomes popular or a few banks open offices in a new city (for example, Houston or Beijing), there is a trend for competitors to rush in. But among the banks with delegations in China during the spring and summer of 1979 were many who recognized the need for a long-term commitment of resources and personnel. In its financial dealings, as in its business selections, China favors "old friends." Prior to 1979 there were several banks in this category, including but not limited to Standard Chartered, Hong Kong-Shanghai, Banque National de Paris, the Bank of Tokyo, First National of Chicago, the Bank of America, Chase Manhattan, and Dresdner, all of whom will be there after 1981. Most of these banks realized that the BOC had been particularly adept at securing excellent terms and conditions, but they were prepared to make initial loans at little profit or even at a loss in order to establish their commitment in China's eyes. These same banks stand ready and willing to lend despite the difficulties involved in the past.

Second, the medium-term prospects for major banks to increase their domestic lending are modest at best. At the same time developing-nation borrowing is becoming heavily saturated. Banks are also frequently coming up against self-imposed or regulatory lending limits to developing-nation borrowers. Nonetheless, the major banks need to place U.S. $20 billion-to-U.S. $30 billion worth of Eurodollars deposited with them each year. Their own high liquidity, combined with these other factors, will make it difficult not to lend, even at wafer-thin margins, to a high-credit-risk and still largely untapped borrower like China.

Third, some profitable lending is being done on a smaller scale in single-bank loans tied to particular projects, especially in export industries and tourism. These small deals are simpler to negotiate, requiring less negotiation and documentation, and some have included terms for setting a schedule or requiring a drawdown. Smaller loans (U.S.$10 million to U.S.$25 million) are also within the borrowing limits set for provincial governments and enterprises under the decentralization programs (for example, recent hotel and aircraft project financings).

In summary, China has lined up excellent sources of commercial credit to back up its low-cost and fixed-rate sources. In the process it has learned a great deal about modern international lending and borrowing, particularly on the Eurodollar markets. By avoiding actually drawing on its lines of credit, it has escaped some of the highest interest rates in three decades. Clearly, China and its foreign bankers have learned fast and benefited from their extreme caution.

NOTES

1. Financial Times, March 3, 1979.
2. Wall Street Journal, May 8, 1979, p. 40.
3. Melinda Liu, "Rock-Bottom Terms Are a Must for Foreigners," Far Eastern Economic Review, September 21, 1979, p. 63.
4. Ibid.; and "Financing the New Customer," Banker 49 (December 1978): 52.
5. Wall Street Journal, February 5, 1979, p. 6, col. 3.
6. Ibid., February 15, 1979, p. 36, col. 6.
7. Economist, March 24, 1979.
8. Wall Street Journal, March 9, 1979, p. 7, col. 1.
9. Far Eastern Economic Review, April 13, 1979, p. 50.
10. "Deals on Ice," China Trade Report 17 (April 1979): 12-13; and "The Uncontrollable 'Stateless Money,'" Far Eastern Economic Review, September 21, 1979, p. 47.
11. Wall Street Journal, May 16, 1979, p. 14, col. 3; and May 18, 1979, p. 27, col. 7.
12. "Chinese Borrowing on the International Capital Markets," International Currency Review 11 (1979): 47-49; and "Deals on Ice," p. 13.
13. New York Times, May 16, 1979, p. 7.
14. For backgrounds, see "The Stateless Money," p. 48; and "China Taking Smaller Arab Loans after Long, Troubled Talks," Asian Wall Street Journal Weekly, February 18, 1980, p. 13, col. 1.
15. Far Eastern Economic Review, February 19, 1979, p. 80; Far Eastern Economic Review, April 13, 1979, p. 50; "Lending to China Hits Eleventh Hour Snafu," South China Morning Post, February 7, 1979; and Mary Goldring, "Tea at the Bank of China," Euromoney 11 (March 1979): 67.
16. "Is China a Non-Event for Bankers? Yes . . . and No," Far Eastern Economic Review, September 19, 1980, pp. 73-74; and China Taking Smaller Arab Loans," p. 13.
17. Charles Smith, "China May Not Use Japan Credits for Plant Imports," Financial Times, March 2, 1981, p. 3, col. 2.
18. Interview in Ta Tung Pao, September 9, 1980, p. 1. Also reported in Foreign Broadcast Information Service, China Report: Economic Affairs, October 7, 1980. See also "Trade with China," Economist, November 10, 1979; and Dick Wilson, "How Banks Work in China," Banker 130 (January 1980): 22.

19. The policy change was announced by Bu-Ming, president of the GAEC, who said, "A special reserve is earmarked in the state plan for repayment of foreign loans and interest." Beijing Review, February 18, 1980, p. 8. The figures for loan repayment appeared in a speech by Wang Binggian at the Third Session of the Fifth National People's Congress and are reported in China Trade Report 18 (November 1980): 4. See also "Is China a Non-Event?" p. 73.

20. Foreign Broadcast Information Service, China Report: Economic Affairs, vol. 92 (October 21, 1980).

21. Provisional Regulations on Foreign Exchange reprinted in the Beijing Review, January 26, 1981, pp. 25-28. They also appear in Appendix B.

22. "Is China a Non-Event?" p. 73.

9

CONCLUSIONS

The international financial system and its banks have a definite role to play in China's rush to modernization. The goals and methods of attaining them have been set on a pragmatic basis. The involvement of foreign lending, almost always present since the Revolution, has now been enlarged. It has emerged from secrecy, then obscurity, into a firm place in the published national budget. The future rates of foreign lending and aid are linked to several economic, as well as political, factors.

China's choice to emphasize economics over politics was itself a political decision. Deng Xioping's vision of massive modernization required annual growth rates of 10 percent in industry and 4 percent in grain production—rates no major nation has ever been able to consistently sustain for the numbers of years called for. Attaining such goals requires careful and considered economic analysis and strategy, but in fact, the goals themselves are based on mere political pronouncements, not realistic assessment of attainable targets. China's politicians are to be credited for their candor in acknowledging that the original plans were too ambitious. The specifics announced in 1978 were first reconsidered, then readjusted, and finally have been redefined altogether. The situation in 1981 is that the commitment to modernization remains, but the rush toward it has been replaced with a step-by-step approach.

Perhaps the most serious barrier to effective implementation of goals is the inability to effectively control domestic overspending. This is a problem in and of itself and it contributes to the very serious newer problem of inflation. Overspending has direct impacts on international trade and borrowing. The domestic deficits have caused cancellation or wholesale rescheduling of many major contracts, most notably involving Japanese sales of steel plants, transportation systems, and oil production units. When local cost elements of projects cannot proceed because of a deficit, foreign contractors and financiers are usually adversely affected. This problem has been enormous and has persisted despite budget cutbacks and political exhortations from the central government to provincial government and enterprise management. The resurgence and rising importance of the domestic banking system is in large part an attempt to regain control, albeit indirectly, over domestic spending. The emerging solutions will be closely watched by international financial institutions, foreign banks, and traders.

The need for improved accuracy in statistic gathering is pressing. Quarterly and midyear figures have, in the past four years, been poor guides to end-of-year results. This is particularly true of financial figures, most especially in capital construction. The problem cannot simply be explained by overspending. Such spending should be reported throughout the year if the methods of gathering statistics are effective and verifiable.

Closely related to these two problems is the need for strengthening of central bank controls. The banking system is being built up, but it is also being decentralized through the revival of old banks and the creation of new financial institutions. The government has recognized since late 1980 the need to find ways to coordinate these institutions' activities through central banking regulations. The solution is made more difficult because a power struggle of sorts is emerging among banks.

While banks are struggling to gain substantial autonomy from the government, they are also vying with each other for independence, growth, and status. The Bank of Construction and the Bank of China (BOC) in particular are trying to establish independence from the People's Bank of China (PBOC). The confusion over just who sets the foreign exchange rate; the issue of PBOC leadership; and the fact that PBOC manager's conferences, and not those of the Construction Bank, have called for the strengthening of central bank controls are all indications of the evolving relative roles of the institutions.

There is considerable ambiguity in banking leadership. The honorary chairman of the BOC is a senior official of the PBOC, as are several other members of the BOC's board of directors. The reverse is also true to a lesser extent. The head of the General Administration of Exchange Control is also the head of the BOC. This interlinking may well weaken the drive for autonomy; it may also reinforce central bank controls.

An answer as to why China has used so little of the commercial bank credit negotiated by it or offered to it must be speculative at this stage. One can, however, suggest several factors likely to have been influential: cost, tradition, political initiative, and political goals.

China, as a financial consumer, measured costs and obviously favored fixed costs over floating rates. Government-supported credits were fixed rate, as were loans from International Financial Organizations (IFOs) and foreign aid. Bonds, if issued, were also likely to be at fixed interest rates. Floating-rate loans tied to the London interbank offered rate (LIBOR) might drop in price, but there was the equal risk that they would rise (which, in fact, occurred during 1980 and 1981) and the fact that LIBOR was much higher than rates available through IFOs, Eximbank, or foreign aid. In 1979 and early 1980 dollar loans backed by the Export Credit Guarantee Department were made available at 7.25 percent and were obviously heavily subsidized over LIBOR (12-14 percent) plus 0.25 percent.

In mid-1979, as China considered its full range of options, the six-month Eurodollar rate was 13.5 percent per annum. It was 17 percent to 18 percent during mid-1981. Mid-1979 rates for other Eurocurrencies varied: 7.5 percent for Dutch guilders, 1.75 for Swiss francs, 8.5 for French francs, 6.0 for Japanese yen, and 11.25 for sterling. China had to weigh the risks and rewards of both interest-rate and exchange-value fluctuations. The choices presented were wide, and the longer the term, the greater the risk. On the whole China has opted to avoid interest-rate risk and to accept instead the risk of exchange-rate fluctuation.

Politics were relevant. China's leaders may have had a political goal of merely proving China's credit status as a first-rate borrower. This could be done by negotiating several agreements on very favorable terms. Winning that goal would not have required taking up the funds available. The final factor considered here is the issue of political initiative. It may well be that leaders intended to make use of loans previously arranged. After the loans were arranged, it started to become apparent that many parts of underlying national development plans were ill-conceived; impossible to efficiently integrate; or would be completed before the requisite raw materials, energy, or transport would be available. For those reasons, or simply out of nervousness over the big step being taken, political leaders were just not willing to make a decision to authorize large-scale borrowing from private banks. However, the political will to act may soon come about. Alternatively, as plans are restructured or stretched out over more years, public-source financing may suffice.

Finally, the confining hand of traditional views has made itself felt. Not only did traditionalists and traditional policies within the Communist party oppose entry into loan negotiations, but these factors must have also operated to make it very difficult to take up the funds offered through successfully concluded loan agreements.

Perhaps the key explanation of China's reluctance to make full use of the credit available to it can be found in its historical experience with world financial markets. For China the risks of manipulation, interference, dependency, and market decline are real. These experiences have made the issues of trade and financial liberalization highly controversial. The debate on those issues cannot be considered closed. The debate over the wisdom of these steps ranges and sways today, just as it did in the 1950s, 1960s, and 1970s. The debate is not over the wisdom of self-reliance, but rather over the wisdom of pragmatic exceptions to the rule. The acceptance of some long-term financing is explained as an exception to the rule caused by a policy decision to speed up the process of self-reliance through rapid modernization. The current pace of modernization exceeds China's ability to earn the requisite foreign exchange. As soon as agricultural and industrial modernization brings increased export production on track, China can be expected to pay off its long-term debts quickly.

The exceptional nature of China's use of foreign financing cannot be overemphasized. China's present leaders differ from their more radical predecessors on this issue, but only because they believe in pragmatic exceptions to Communist dogma. The possibility must also be faced that, as so often before, yet another in a series of dramatic changes in China's internal politics will occur, which will wipe out overnight the exception to the rule. In June 1980 the fundamental policy was restated to Western business leaders by a senior BOC official.

China will accept and utilize foreign funds according to the plan and import urgently needed advanced technology and equipment on a selective basis with the proviso of being able to stick to independence and self-reliance. It is a major policy which will be persistently pursued by our government for a long time to come.

AFTERWORD

It has been possible to update and change some material written in June 1981.

RESERVE AND GOLD HOLDINGS

In July 1981 China began regular publication of limited monetary statistics. It announced foreign exchange reserves of U.S.$2,262 million at year-end 1980 and gold holdings of 12.3 million troy ounces (valued at approximately U.S.$4.92 billion, if gold is arbitrarily taken to be worth U.S.$400 an ounce. (See Appendix C.) Total reserves approximate U.S.$7.0 billion to U.S.$7.5 billion in mid-1981. This is considerably higher than the U.S.$6 billion figure given by Vice-Premier Yao Yilin on November 7, 1980 (cited in Chapter 1). The value of gold holdings appears to correspond with that statement, but the value of foreign exchange reserves is surprisingly high, given the deficits and borrowings of 1979 and 1980. After 1980 China's holdings at the third quarter of 1981 had increased further and stood at U.S.$3.82 billion and 12.8 million ounces of gold.

FOREIGN MONETARY POLICY

In its Annual Report on Exchange Arrangements and Exchange Restrictions: 1981, the International Monetary Fund (IMF) footnotes China's introduction of a split rate for exchange of renminbi (RMB). The report indicates that the rate is formed by adding an "equalization price" to the official rate to balance export and import profits and losses. It applies to all national enterprises and corporations engaged in trade, as well as to receipts and expenditures in foreign exchange for trade-related transactions in invisibles, such as shipping and insurance. The official rate is still applicable to other invisibles and for all settlements with nonresidents denominated in RMB.

The IMF's report also indicates that the experimental exchange markets, described in Chapter 1 above, do not operate at floating market rates. It states that the internal fixed exchange rate of RMB 2.8 per U.S.$1 operates with the Bank of China (BOC) collecting a broker commission of from 0.1 percent to 0.3 percent on both sides of the transaction.

THE BANKING SYSTEM

Considerable groundwork has been done, and apparently, the fundamental decision has been made to introduce a nationwide industrial-commercial bank. It was thought that the first few branches of this operation would be set up by late 1981. In April plans for these operations were delayed indefinitely.[1] One problem causing the delay was internal disagreement over the degree of centralized control. The People's Bank of China (PBOC) appears to be involved in a semiofficial campaign to introduce a strong central banking system, with the PBOC at the top and all other banks under it as "specialized banks."[2]

Other problems were primarily technical, involving the source and the amount of funding for the new bank and the source of trained staff. In November 1981 it became known that the new bank was primarily to be an investment banking operation, which would be set up in conjunction with the World Bank's plans for training the Chinese in appraising borrowers and in preparing lending guidelines, procedures, and operation plans. Such programs are similar to those set up by the World Bank in other countries.[3]

Some of the technical problems have been considerably reduced by two decisions. First, the investment bank will operate as a subsidiary of the Construction Bank of China, which is already in charge of capital-construction investment. That bank will provide some of the funding and considerable staff. Second, funding will come from the World Bank and directly from the Chinese government in a form of capital grant.

In an end-of-the-year announcement, Xinhua News Agency reported that the China Investment Bank had been established along the above lines. Its capital was equivalent to about U.S.$2.7 billion and the bank will seek long- and medium-term loans from the International Financial Organizations (IFOs). Its chairman is Vice-Finance Minister Wu Bashan, who also heads the Construction Bank.

OVERSEAS BONDS AND DEBENTURES

The first overseas bond issue since the 1949 Revolution now appears imminent. It was mentioned above that a private placement of bonds in the amount of ¥10 billion (Japanese) was proposed in early 1980. It was hoped that the issue would be placed by the summer of 1981. However, the Japanese Ministry of Finance was reluctant to permit speedy issuance during 1980 and 1981. The ministry was insistent that China's bond issue would have to wait in line behind other earlier borrowers and that only one such issue was being allowed a month. It was unlikely that the bond issue could take place before the spring of 1982, but the Ministry of Finance changed its mind in late 1981 and approved placement of the issue for December 1981. The interest rate is expected to be 0.2 percent to 0.8 percent above the long-term prime rate for yen—about 8.5 percent in October 1981.

Several Chinese provinces have continued negotiations with Japanese underwriters over yen-denominated issues. Many more provinces have made it clear that they plan private placements of bonds with wealthy investors in Hong Kong. Guizhou Province is most advanced and wants to raise HK$1 billion (U.S.$169 million) to finance coal exploration. The proposed issue would be placed with about 15 prominent Hong Kong families and have a maturity of from 10 to 12 years, at an interest rate of 8 percent to 8.5 percent per annum. Shanxi, Shandong, and Henan provinces are also expected to attempt bond issues for coal exploration. Both Guangdong and Guizhou provinces are also discussing bond issues for rail modernization. The latter would be linked to subsidized coal exports for purchasers of the bonds.

Fujian Province is believed to be close to announcing a major private bond placement in Hong Kong, and possibly in Japan in early 1982.[4] The first stage will be a U.S.$11.4 million debt issue denominated in RMB but sold in Hong Kong and overseas through the BOC's Hong Kong branch. Purchasers will have to acquire RMB with which to pay the notes or bonds, and thus China's foreign exchange earnings will be increased. Interest will be paid in RMB, but on maturity (8, 10, or 12 years) bondholders will be paid half of the face value in foreign currency. The debt will carry an annual interest of 6 percent, 7 percent, or 8 percent. The issue will be guaranteed by the Fuzhou branch of the BOC and issued by the Fujian Investment and Enterprise Corporation. This is to be followed by a ¥5 billion yen-denominated bond issue in Japan in early 1982. That will also be issued by Fujian Investment and Enterprise Corporation and underwritten by Sanyo Securities Company and the Bank of Tokyo.

OIL RECEIPTS

In mid to late 1981 a variety of sources, including the World Bank, predicted that unless Chinese oil production policies were changed, production would continue to decline some 20 percent to 25 percent by 1985 from the current 2 million barrels a day. After 20 years of production output in existing fields has now clearly peaked. This is true despite three satisfactory test drillings in the Bohai Gulf region by the joint venture between Japan and China's national oil companies.

As of this writing no new capital-spending programs, which would increase energy investment, have been announced by the Chinese government. New oil exploration legislation, considered a prerequisite to foreign oil company participation, has not been announced. The slump in oil production has also affected the petrochemical and agricultural industries, as well as direct export commitments to Japan, Hong Kong, and Malaysia. In the first half of 1981, for example, the production of nitrogenous fertilizer fell 5.252 percent from 1980 and production of insecticides plunged 20.5 percent.[5]

GOVERNMENTAL CREDIT AGREEMENTS

The U.S. Export-Import Bank (Eximbank) has arranged its first export credit facility for China. In October 1981 the bank pledged U.S.$28.4 million on terms believed to be the most favorable allowed under the Organization for Economic Cooperation and Development's "gentlemen's agreement." Shortly thereafter First National Bank of Chicago announced that it was providing $3.7 million to the BOC for the use of Chinese machine-building companies under a guarantee agreement issued by Eximbank. The Austrian government's export credit agency has also financed a straight U.S.$5 million export credit for oil refining equipment to be used by a Beijing municipally owned company.

INTERNATIONAL FINANCIAL ORGANIZATIONS

On January 1, 1981, the IMF held RMB 3.47 billion, equivalent to China's quota of SDR (Special Drawing Rights) 1.8 billion. By July 31, 1981, the IMF's holdings of RMB had increased to 4.5 billion (SDR 2.25 billion) indicating a substantial net borrowing of foreign currency by China. China had paid in approximately RMB 1.5 billion to the fund for its standby withdrawal ("purchase") of SDR 450 million (cited in chapter 7).[6]

SYNDICATED BORROWING

The year 1981 has seen a dramatic decrease in publicly announced Eurocurrency bank credits for China. The total in 1979 was U.S.$3,395 million, only U.S.$131 million in 1980, and just U.S.$50 million through November 1981. However, during 1981 the total of credits from IFOs reached U.S.$1,294 million by the first half of 1981 alone, all at very low or virtually interest-free rates. The Chinese government permitted a subsidiary of the Beijing municipality, Yan Shan Petrochemical General Corporation (YSP), to sign a syndicated credit involving payment by YSP of both commitment and management fees.[7] The U.S.$50.2 million credit was arranged by Amex Bank Limited, the merchant banking subsidiary of American Express International Banking Corporation. Working with its Italian subsidiary, Amex Bank put together a syndicate of lenders to finance the export of Italian machinery for refinery operations of YSP.

The credit is a hybrid between an export credit and commercial loan. YSP will pay only 7.5 percent annual interest, the agreed-upon rate for export credits when YSP contracted to buy the Italian-made machinery, and Italy's export credit agency will pay the participating banks the difference between that rate and the London interbank offered rate (LIBOR), plus 0.875 percent. Participating banks will also receive management fees, paid in Italian lire.

Payment is arranged by the YSP issuing promissory notes to the Italian manufacturer, who will resell the promissory notes to the banks as deliveries are made. The Chinese borrower pays a commitment fee of 0.5 percent on the notes to be released progressively through January 1984.

The arrangement is an innovative one and represents a significant breakthrough in the borrowing practices of Chinese entities up to that date. It is the first reported syndicated credit in which the Chinese borrower has agreed to both commitment and management fees. Perhaps the most significant aspect of the transaction is that, although Italy's export credit agency is paying the interest differential, it is not guaranteeing the loan. The credit risk has been assumed directly by the banks, although the Beijing Economic Development Corporation, a state-owned entity, is the nominal guarantor. In late December 1981 Japan's foreign minister announced signing of an agreement to lend China U.S.$1.37 billion at interest rates subsidized by Japan. One portion, U.S.$320 million, will be a syndicated commercial credit that China is obligated to draw down by 1983.

The progress in bond sale proposals and the continued trends in relation to syndicated credits are significant for a number of reasons. It was believed that Japan's minister of finance was delaying the China International Trust and Investment Corporation's issue in part because of the annoyance over China's cancellation of construction contracts with Japanese enterprises. Although that issue was not resolved by late 1981, it is a significant sign of the Japanese government's continued goodwill toward China that the earlier-than-expected issuance of the bonds was approved. Of overall significance is the continued search by Chinese enterprises, through bond issues and hybrid syndicated loans—such as the Italian credit described above—to avoid paying floating interest rates tied to world markets. Despite continued ample access to syndicated credits, China consistently prefers to use virtually any alternative to borrowing at money market floating rates. China also continues to borrow in foreign currencies that have been cautiously selected for their stability. Whether those policies and selections are correct in the long term remains to be seen.

NOTES

1. "China Delays Plan for Industrial Bank," Far Eastern Economic Review, April 10, 1981, p. 8.

2. Zhang Enhua, "On Banking Reform," Beijing Review, July 20, 1981, pp. 24-27.

3. Dinah Lee, "Trade Follows the Loans," Far Eastern Economic Review, May 29, 1981, p. 50; and Wall Street Journal, November 2, 1981, p. 18.

4. "China Province Seeks Funds from Overseas through Bond Issue," Asian Wall Street Journal Weekly, November 16, 1981, p. 4.

5. Asian Wall Street Journal Weekly, August 17, 1981, p. 2.

6. International Monetary Fund, Financial Statements of the General Department and the SDR Department and Accounts Administered by the International Monetary Fund, quarter ended July 31, 1981.

7. E. S. Browning, "China Turns to Syndicate to Pay for Italian Imports," Asian Wall Street Journal Weekly, July 13, 1981, p. 6.

APPENDIX A

ARTICLES OF ASSOCIATION OF THE BANK OF CHINA

CHAPTER 1

General Provisions

Article 1

The Bank of China is a state-owned socialist enterprise and is the specialized foreign exchange bank of the People's Republic of China.

Article 2

The functions of the Bank of China are: to raise, utilize, accumulate and manage foreign exchange funds, to engage in all kinds of foreign exchange business, and to participate in international financial activities for the purpose of rendering service to the modernization of China's socialist construction.

Article 3

The Head Office of the Bank of China shall be established in Beijing. To meet the needs of business, the Bank may set up branches, subbranches and representative offices at places of commercial and financial importance both in China and abroad.

Approved by the State Council on September 22, 1980.

CHAPTER 2

Capital

Article 4

The authorized capital of the Bank of China shall be Renminbi 1,000 million Yuan.

CHAPTER 3

Business

Article 5

The Bank of China shall engage in and handle when entrusted, the following kinds of business:

1. International settlements in connection with foreign trade and non-trade transactions.
2. International inter-bank deposits and loans.
3. Overseas Chinese remittances and other international remittances.
4. Deposits and loans in foreign currencies; and, with the approval of the People's Bank of China, deposits and loans in Renminbi which relate to foreign exchange business.
5. Buying and selling of foreign exchange (including foreign currencies).
6. Buying and selling of gold in the international markets.
7. Organizing and participating in international syndicated loans.
8. Investing singly by itself or jointly with others in banking business, finance companies and other enterprises in foreign countries and in the Hongkong and Macao regions.
9. Issuing bonds and securities in foreign currencies with the authorization of the State.
10. Providing trust and advisory services.
11. Engaging in other kinds of banking business approved or entrusted by the State.

Article 6

The Bank of China shall participate in international financial meetings with the authorization of the State.

Article 7

Branches and offices of the Bank of China set up in foreign countries and in the Hongkong and Macao regions may engage in all kinds of banking business which are permitted by local laws and regulations.

CHAPTER 4

Organization

Article 8

The Bank of China shall have a Board of Directors consisting of an honorary Chairman, a Chairman, and a number of Vice Chairmen, Managing Directors and Directors, all to be appointed by the State Council.

Article 9

The functions of the Board of Directors of the Bank of China are as follows:

1. To examine and determine the business policies and plans of the Bank.
2. To receive and examine the President's reports on the work of the Bank.
3. To examine and approve the Bank's annual financial statements and proposals for the distribution of profits.
4. To appoint and remove high officials of the Bank.
5. To consider and determine the setting up and closing down of branches, sub-branches and offices of the Bank in China and abroad.
6. To consider and examine other important matters relating to the Bank.

Article 10

The Bank of China shall have a Board of Supervisors consisting of a Chief Supervisor and a number of Supervisors all to be appointed by the State Council.

Article 11

The functions of the Board of Supervisors are as follows:

1. To supervise the Bank's implementation of the policies, laws, and orders of the State as well as the Bank's business policies.
2. To examine the annual financial statements of the Bank.
3. To investigate matters of a serious nature and submit opinions on ways of dealing with them.

Article 12

The Bank of China shall have a President and a number of Vice Presidents to be nominated by the Chairman of the Board of Directors who shall, with the approval of the Board of Directors, submit his nominations to the State Council for appointments.

Article 13

The President of the Bank of China shall be responsible for the overall operation and administration of the Bank and shall submit to the Board of Directors periodic reports on the work of the Bank. The Vice Presidents shall assist the President in his work.

CHAPTER 5

Meetings

Article 14

A meeting of the Board of Directors shall be held once a year and is to be convoked by the Chairman. A meeting of the Board of

Supervisors shall be held once a year and is to be convoked by the Chief Supervisor. If necessary, the convocation of the aforesaid meetings may take place in advance or be postponed; and the Chairman of the Board of Directors may also convoke joint meetings of the Directors and Supervisors.

Article 15

Meetings of the Board of Directors, meetings of the Board of Supervisors, and joint meetings of the Directors and Supervisors shall all require a quorum of more than two thirds of their respective members (including proxies). All resolutions, to be effective, must be passed by more than one half of the persons attending the meetings.

CHAPTER 6

Addendum

Article 16

The present Articles of Association shall come into force upon the approval of the State Council. The same applies to amendments.

APPENDIX B

PROVISIONAL REGULATIONS FOR EXCHANGE CONTROL OF THE PEOPLE'S REPUBLIC OF CHINA

Following is the full text of the provisional regulations for exchange control of the People's Republic of China promulgated by the State Council on December 18, 1980. They came into force on March 1, 1981.

CHAPTER 1

General Provisions

Article 1

These provisional regulations are formulated for the purpose of strengthening exchange control, increasing national foreign exchange income and economizing on foreign exchange expenditure so as to expedite the national economic growth and safeguard the rights and interests of the country.

All foreign exchange income and expenditure, the issuance and circulation of all kinds of payment instruments in foreign currency, dispatch and carriage into and out of the People's Republic of China of foreign exchange, precious metals and payment instruments in foreign currency shall be governed by these regulations.

Article 2

Foreign exchange herein mentioned refers to:

1. Foreign currencies, including banknotes, coins, etc.
2. Securities in foreign currency, including government bonds, treasury bills, corporate bonds and debentures, shares, interest and dividend coupons, etc.

3. Instruments payable in foreign currency, including bills, drafts, cheques, bank deposit certificates, postal savings certificates, etc.

4. Other foreign exchange funds.

Article 3

The People's Republic of China pursues the policy of centralized control and unified management of foreign exchange by the state.

The administrative organ in charge of exchange control of the People's Republic of China is the State General Administration of Exchange Control (SGAEC) and its branch offices.

The specialized foreign exchange bank of the People's Republic of China is the Bank of China. No other financial institution shall engage in foreign exchange business, unless approved by the SGAEC.

Article 4

All Chinese and foreign organizations and individuals in the People's Republic of China must, unless otherwise stipulated by law or decree or in these regulations, sell their foreign exchange proceeds to the Bank of China. Any foreign exchange required is to be sold to them by the Bank of China in accordance with the quota approved by the state or with relevant regulations.

The circulation, use and mortgage of foreign currency in the People's Republic of China are prohibited. Unauthorized sales and purchases of foreign exchange and unlawfully seizing possession of foreign exchange in whatever ways and by whatever means are prohibited.

CHAPTER 2

Exchange Control Relating to State Organizations and Collective Economic Units

Article 5

Foreign exchange income and expenditure of state organs, armed forces units, nongovernmental bodies, educational institutions, state enterprises, government establishments, and urban and rural collective economic units in China (hereinafter referred to as domestic organizations) are all subject to control according to plan.

Domestic organizations are permitted to retain a proportion of their foreign exchange receipts in accordance with relevant regulations.

Article 6

Unless approved by the SGAEC or its branch offices, domestic organizations shall not: possess foreign exchange; deposit foreign exchange abroad; offset foreign exchange expenditure against foreign exchange income; or use the foreign exchange belonging to state organs stationed abroad or Chinese enterprises and establishments resident in foreign countries or in the Xianggang (Hongkong) and Aomen (Macao) regions, by way of borrowing or acquisition.

Article 7

Unless approved by the State Council, domestic organizations shall not issue securities with foreign exchange value inside or outside China.

Article 8

Departments under the State Council and people's governments of various provinces, municipalities and autonomous regions shall compile annual overall plans for domestic organizations under their respective jurisdiction whereby loans may be accepted from banks or enterprises in foreign countries or in the Xianggang (Hongkong) and Aomen (Macao) regions. These plans shall be submitted to the SGAEC and the Foreign Investment Control Commission for examination and forwarding to the State Council for approval.

The procedure for examining and approving individual borrowings shall be prescribed separately.

Article 9

The portion of foreign exchange retained by domestic organizations, non-trade foreign exchange and foreign exchange under compensatory trade received in advance for later payments, funds borrowed in convertible foreign currency, and other foreign exchange held with the approval of the SGAEC or its branch offices, must be placed in foreign currency deposit accounts or foreign currency quota accounts to be opened with the Bank of China, and must be used within the prescribed scope and be subject to the supervision of the Bank of China.

Article 10

When domestic organizations import or export goods, the banks handling the transactions shall check their foreign exchange receipts and payments either against the import or export licenses duly verified by the customs or against the customs declaration forms for imports or exports.

Article 11

State organs stationed abroad must use foreign exchange according to the plan approved by the state.

The operating profits of enterprises and establishments in foreign countries or in the Xianggang (Hongkong) and Aomen (Macao) regions must, except the portion kept locally as working funds according to the plan approved by the state, be transferred back on scheduled time and be sold to the Bank of China.

No Chinese organization stationed abroad is permitted to keep foreign exchange for domestic organizations without authorization.

Article 12

Delegations and work-groups sent temporarily to foreign countries or to the Xianggang (Hongkong) and Aomen (Macao) regions must use foreign exchange according to their respective specific plans, and must, upon their return, promptly transfer back to China their surplus foreign exchange to be checked by and sold to the Bank of China.

Foreign exchange earned in their various business activities by the delegations and work-groups referred to in the above paragraph and by members thereof, must be promptly transferred back to China and must not be kept abroad without the approval of the SGAEC or its branch offices.

CHAPTER 3

Exchange Control Relating to Individuals

Article 13

Foreign exchange remitted from foreign countries or from the Xianggang (Hongkong) and Aomen (Macao) regions to Chinese or foreign nationals or stateless persons residing in China must be sold to the Bank of China, except the portion retained as permitted by the state.

Article 14

Chinese and foreign nationals and stateless persons residing in China are permitted to keep in their own possession foreign exchange already in China.

The foreign exchange referred to in the above paragraph shall not, without authorization, be carried or sent out of China either in person or by others or by post. If the owners wish to sell the foreign exchange, they must sell it to the Bank of China and are permitted to retain a portion thereof as convertible foreign currency according to the percentage prescribed by the state.

Article 15

When foreign exchange that has been kept in foreign countries or in the Xianggang (Hongkong) and Aomen (Macao) regions by Chinese residents in China prior to the founding of the People's Republic of China, by overseas Chinese prior to their returning to and settling down in China, by Xianggang (Hongkong) and Aomen (Macao) compatriots prior to their returning to and settling down in their home places, is transferred to China, the owners are permitted to retain a portion thereof as convertible foreign currency according to the percentage prescribed by the state.

Article 16

When foreign exchange belonging personally to individuals sent to work or study in foreign countries or in the Xianggang

(Hongkong) and Aomen (Macao) regions is remitted or brought back to China, the owners returning after completion of their missions are permitted to retain the entire amount as convertible foreign currency.

Article 17

The percentages of foreign exchange retention permitted under Articles 13, 14 and 15 of these regulations shall be prescribed separately.

Foreign exchange retained by individuals as permitted under Articles 13, 14, 15 and 16 of these regulations must be deposited with the Bank of China. These foreign exchange deposits may be sold to the Bank of Chima or remitted out of China through the Bank of China, or taken out of China against certification by the Bank of China. It is however not permitted, without authorization, to carry or send deposit certificates out of China either in person or by others or by post.

Article 18

Foreign exchange remitted or brought into China from foreign countries or from the Xianggang (Hongkong) and Aomen (Macao) regions by foreign nationals coming to China, by overseas Chinese and Xianggang (Hongkong) and Aomen (Macao) compatriots returning for a short stay, by foreign experts, technicians, staff members and workers engaged to work in domestic organizations, and by foreign students and trainees, may be kept in their own possession, or sold to or deposited with the Bank of China, or remitted or taken out of China.

Article 19

Chinese and foreign nationals and stateless persons residing in China may apply to the local branch offices of the SGAEC for the purchase of foreign exchange to be remitted or taken out of China. When approved, the required foreign exchange will be sold to the applicants by the Bank of China.

When foreign experts, technicians, staff members and workers engaged to work in domestic organizations require foreign exchange to be remitted or taken out of China, the Bank of China will deal with their applications in accordance with the stipulations in the contracts or agreements.

CHAPTER 4

Exchange Control Relating to Foreign Representations in China and Their Personnel

Article 20

Foreign exchange remitted or brought into China from foreign countries or from the Xianggang (Hongkong) and Aomen (Macao) regions by foreign diplomatic missions, consulates, official commercial offices, offices of international organizations and non-governmental bodies resident in China, diplomatic officials and consuls as well as members of the permanent staff of the above units, may be kept in their own possession, or sold to or deposited with the Bank of China, or remitted or taken out of China.

Article 21

The conversion into foreign currency, if required, of visa and certification fees received in Renminbi from Chinese citizens by foreign diplomatic missions and consulates in China, is subject to approval by the SGAEC or its branch offices.

CHAPTER 5

Exchange Control Relating to Enterprises with Overseas Chinese Capital, Enterprises with Foreign Capital, and Chinese and Foreign Joint Ventures and Their Personnel

Article 22

All foreign exchange receipts of enterprises with overseas Chinese capital, enterprises with foreign capital and Chinese and foreign joint ventures, must be deposited with the Bank of China, and all their foreign exchange disbursements must be paid from their foreign exchange deposit accounts.

The enterprises referred to in the above paragraph must submit periodic reports and statements of their foreign exchange business to the SGAEC or its branch offices, all of which are empowered to inspect their activities in respect to their foreign exchange receipts and payments.

Article 23

Except where otherwise approved by the SGAEC or its branch offices, Renminbi should in all cases be used in the settlement of accounts between enterprises with overseas Chinese capital, enterprises with foreign capital, Chinese and foreign joint ventures and other enterprises and individuals residing in the People's Republic of China.

Article 24

Enterprises with overseas Chinese capital, enterprises with foreign capital and foreign partners in Chinese and foreign joint ventures may apply to the Bank of China for remitting abroad their net profits after tax as well as other legitimate earnings by debiting the foreign exchange deposit accounts of the enterprises concerned.

The enterprises and foreign partners referred to in the above paragraph should apply to the SGAEC or its branch offices for transferring foreign exchange capital abroad by debiting the foreign exchange deposit accounts of the enterprises concerned.

Article 25

An amount not exceeding 50 per cent of their net wages and other legitimate earnings after tax may be remitted or taken out of China in foreign currency by staff members and workers of foreign nationality and those from the Xianggang (Hongkong) and Aomen (Macao) regions employed by enterprises with overseas Chinese capital, enterprises with foreign capital and Chinese and foreign joint ventures.

Article 26

Enterprises with overseas Chinese capital, enterprises with foreign capital and Chinese and foreign joint ventures which wind up operations in accordance with legal procedure, should be responsible for the liquidation within the scheduled period of their outstanding liabilities and taxes due in China, under the joint supervision of the relevant departments in charge and the SGAEC or its branch offices.

CHAPTER 6

Control Relating to Carrying Foreign Exchange, Precious Metals and Payment Instruments in Foreign Currency Into and Out of China

Article 27

No restriction as to the amount is imposed on the carrying into China of foreign exchange, precious metals and objects made from them, but declaration to the customs is required at the place of entry.

To carry foreign exchange out of China or to carry out of China the foreign exchange previously brought in shall be permitted by the customs against certification by the Bank of China or against the original declaration form at the time of entry.

To carry out of China precious metals and objects made from them or to carry out of China the precious metals and objects made from them previously brought in shall be permitted by the customs according to the specific circumstances as prescribed by government regulations or against the original declaration form at the time of entry.

Article 28

Renminbi traveller's cheques, traveller's letters of credit and other Renminbi payment instruments convertible into foreign currency may be brought into China against declaration to the customs, and taken out of China against certification by the Bank of China or against the original declaration form at the time of entry.

Article 29

Unless otherwise approved by the SGAEC or its branch offices, the carrying or sending out of China either in person or by others or by post of the following documents and securities held by Chinese residing in China is not permitted: bonds, debentures, share certificates issued abroad; title deeds for real estate abroad; documents or deeds necessary in dealing with creditor's right or owner's right to possession regarding inheritance, real estate and other foreign exchange assets.

Article 30

The carrying or sending out of China of Renminbi cheques, drafts, passbooks, deposit certificates and other Renminbi instruments held by Chinese or foreign nationals or stateless persons residing in China, is not permitted, either in person or by others or by post.

CHAPTER 7

Supplementary Provisions

Article 31

All units and individuals have the right to report any violation of these regulations. Reward shall be given to such units or individuals according to the merit of the report. Violators shall be penalized by the SGAEC, its branch offices or by the departments of public security, or by the departments of administration of industry and commerce, or by the customs. According to the seriousness of the offence, the penalties may take the form of compulsory exchange of the foreign currency for Renminbi, or fine or confiscation of the properties or both, or punishment by judicial authorities according to law.

Article 32

The exchange control regulations for special economic zones, for trade in border areas, and for personal dealings between inhabitants across the border shall be formulated by the people's governments of the provinces, municipalities and autonomous regions concerned in the spirit of these regulations and in the light of specific local conditions, and shall be enforced upon the approval of the State Council.

Article 33

Detailed provisions for the enforcement of these regulations shall be formulated by the SGAEC.

Article 34

These regulations shall come into force on March 1, 1981.

APPENDIX C

CHINA'S OFFICIAL MONETARY STATISTICS, 1979-80

TABLE C.1

Receipts and Payments of State Credit Funds
(renminbi: million yuan)

Items	End of 1979	End of 1980
Deposits	134,004	165,864
Deposits by enterprises	46,891	57,309
Deposits by the treasury	14,868	16,202
Capital construction funds	13,130	17,175
Deposits by government departments and organizations	18,488	22,945
Savings deposits in cities and towns	20,256	28,249
Deposits in rural areas	20,371	23,984
Deposits by international monetary institutions		3,427
Currency in circulation	26,771	34,620
Bank's working funds	42,788	47,733
Bank's surplus	4,945	2,719
Other	7,752	8,063
Total credit funds	216,260	262,426
Loans	203,963	241,430
To industrial production enterprises	36,309	43,158
To industrial supply and marketing enterprises and materials supply departments	24,212	23,603
Commercial loans	123,225	143,702
Short- and medium-term loans for buying equipment	792	5,550
Industrial and commercial loans to urban collective and individual enterprises	5,751	7,829
For earnest money	698	788
To state farms	686	940
To rural communes and production brigades	12,290	15,860
Gold purchases	1,216	1,216
Foreign exchange purchases	2,058	-847
Balances with the International Monetary Fund		3,604
Money advanced to the Ministry of Finance	9,023	17,023
Total credit funds used	216,260	262,426

Source: Beijing Review, July 20, 1981, pp. 21-22.

TABLE C.2

Deposits and Loans by Rural Credit Cooperatives
(renminbi: million yuan)

Items	End of 1979	End of 1980
Total deposits	21,588	27,234
Deposits by communes and production brigades	9,833	10,548
Deposits by commune- and brigade-run enterprises	2,193	2,947
Deposits by commune members	7,843	11,703
Other	1,719	2,036
Total loans	4,754	8,164
Agricultural loans to communes and production brigades	2,254	3,454
Loans to commune- and brigade-run enterprises	1,415	3,111
Loans to individual commune members	1,085	1,599

Source: Beijing Review, July 20, 1981, pp. 21-22.

TABLE C.3

Exchange Rate, Foreign Exchange, and Gold Reserves
(in yuan)

Items	1979	1980
Renminbi exchange rate for one SDR (year-end rate)	1.9710	1.9517
Renminbi exchange rate for one U.S. dollar (year-end rate)	1.4962	1.5303
Renminbi exchange rate for one U.S. dollar (average rate for the year)	1.5549	1.4984
Gold and foreign exchange reserves		
Foreign exchange (million U.S. dollars)	2,154	2,262
Gold (million troy ounces)	12.8	12.8

Source: Beijing Review, July 20, 1981, pp. 21-22.

GLOSSARY

ASIA DOLLAR MARKET. The money market for U.S. dollars centered in Asia. See also EURODOLLAR and EURODOLLAR MARKET.

BANK DRAFT. A check drawn by one bank on another bank. The bank draft is customarily used where it is necessary for a customer to provide funds that are payable at a bank at some distant location.

BILL OF EXCHANGE (DRAFT BILL). A negotiable draft drawn by an exporter on an importer at sight or over a specified credit period. The draft covers the contract price of goods in a trade transaction. In trade with China, bills of exchange are generally drawn under a letter of credit opened in the exporter's favor.

BUYER'S CREDITS. Credits granted directly to a foreign buyer by banks or other credit institutions, enabling the buyer to pay cash to the supplier for imports. In Japan, medium- and long-term buyer's credits are known as "overseas direct loans."

CLEARING BANK. One of the commercial bank group that carries out nearly all commercial banking in the United Kingdom.

COMANAGER. The major participant in a new bond issue or syndicated loan who underwrites or lends a relatively large por-

---

Based on glossaries in Phillips and Drew, A Guide to the Eurobond Market (London: Phillips and Drew, 1979); Suzanne F. Porter, East-West Trade Financing (Washington, D.C.: U.S. Department of Commerce, 1976); and "A Countertrade Glossary," China Business Review, July-August 1981, p. 31.

tion of the issue or loan and may receive a portion of the management fee.

COMPENSATION TRADE. A sale of foreign equipment or technology to a Chinese firm under which the seller is paid in whole or in part with products or output resulting from the acquired equipment or technology. The term is sometimes used to describe arrangements whereby Chinese workers process imported (raw) materials. See also COUNTERTRADE.

CONVERTIBLE CURRENCY. A currency that can be freely exchanged for foreign currencies or gold in the open market. Limited convertibility applies to the changing of one currency into another with government permission.

COUNTERTRADE. Any transaction that links capital imports to future delivery of exports, normally either done as compensation trade or counterpurchase.

CULTURAL REVOLUTION. A popular campaign from 1966 to 1969 involving large masses of people challenging many of the trends in education, industrial management, banking, law, agricultural development, and general economic development strategy. The campaigns turned violent and abusive, most notoriously through the activities of the student Red Guards movement.

DOCUMENTARY CREDITS. Financing, usually by letter of credit, that requires that the trade documents (invoice, bill of lading, insurance certificate, and others) specified in the letter of credit accompany bills of exchange when they are discounted at a commercial bank. See also LETTER OF CREDIT.

DRAFT. See BILL OF EXCHANGE; BANK DRAFT.

EUROBOND. A special type of security representing debt, underwritten by multinational syndicates and floated simultaneously in several countries.

EURODOLLAR. U.S. dollar owned by foreigners and placed on deposit in banks or similar institutions outside the United States, principally in Europe. Such deposits are available for lending to corporations and other banks and can be used to finance trade.

EURODOLLAR MARKET. The money market for U.S. dollars located outside the United States of America. Originally, it was centered in Europe, hence the appellation "Euro." At present, the term applies worldwide. Markets in other currencies that have developed outside their domestic center also carry the "Euro" prefix (e.g., Eurodeutsche mark, Eurosterling, Euroyen). See also ASIA DOLLAR MARKET.

FLOATING RATE NOTE. An issue carrying a variable rate of interest.

FOUR MODERNIZATIONS. A plan or campaign begun in 1978 to promote rapid economic development by focusing resources in four key areas—agriculture, science and technology, defense, and industry—in order to modernize by the end of the century.

GANG OF FOUR. Consisted of the widow of Mao, and three other politiburo members associated with a radical faction of the Communist party who strongly favored a revival of the upheavals of the Cultural Revolution. After their arrest in 1977 and through 1979 they were the focus of a large-scale campaign to criticize the ideas they stood for, and albeit indirectly, the "mistakes" of Chairman Mao.

GREAT LEAP FORWARD. A period of intense political and economic upheaval and experimentation from 1958 to 1960 involving reorganization of agriculture, medicine, education, decentralization of government, and the roles of industry and the sexes.

HARD CURRENCY. The term hard is a carry-over from the days when sound money was freely convertible into hard metal, such as gold. The term is used today to describe a currency that has a sound value, and which is generally acceptable at face value internationally.

INVESTMENT BANK. Firm that originates, underwrites, and distributes new security issues of corporations and government agencies. A syndicate of investment banking firms is organized for underwriting and distribution of most security issues. If the amount of capital sought is large enough to prevent one investment banking firm's undertaking the risk of purchasing the entire issue, the investment bank that initiates the issue with the corporation organizes a group of investment bankers to divide the liability for the purchase, with the originator acting as manager of the group.

JOINT VENTURE. Two companies combine to form a third company to carry on a manufacturing or service business. Each founder owns a share of the capital but may agree to sell out to the partner over a number of years or upon expiration of a term of years.

LETTER OF CREDIT. A bank-to-bank facility extended by an exporter's bank at the request of an importer's bank whereby the former agrees to accept for discounting up to a fixed limit and under terms specified in the letter of credit, bills of exchange, or promissory notes drawn in favor of the exporter against the importer. Through the issuance of such letters, a bank pledges its credit on behalf of its customers and thereby facilitates the transaction of business between parties who may not be otherwise acquainted with each other. The drafts may be payable upon presentation to the bank that issued the credit or at some later time, as fixed by the terms of the credit. The letter of credit may be sent by the issuing bank or its customer to the beneficiary, or the terms of the credit may be transmitted through a correspondent bank. In this case, the correspondent bank may add its guarantee (confirmation) to that of the issuing bank, depending on the arrangements made between the seller and the buyer. When such a guarantee is added, the letter is described as a confirmed credit. Letters of credit may be revocable or irrevocable, depending on whether the issuing bank reserves the right to cancel the credit prior to its expiration date.

LIBOR. London interbank offered rate. Frequently used to refer to the interest rate charged on six-month Eurodollar deposits.

MERCHANT BANK. The English term for what is generally known as an investment bank in American banking language. In the United States the term also indicates an acceptance house or dealer in commercial paper, for example, bills of exchange or drafts.

SOCIALIST. As used in this publication, socialist refers to state trading countries with centrally planned economies. These include Bulgaria, Czechoslovakia, the German Democratic Republic, Hungary, Poland, Romania, the Soviet Union, and the People's Republic of China.

SPREAD. (1) The difference between a market maker's buying and selling price. (2) In the case of floating rate notes, the difference between the London interbank offered rate (LIBOR) and the coupon on the floating rate note.

SUPPLIER'S CREDITS. Credits granted by a supplier (exporter), usually through commercial banks, to a foreign buyer.

BIBLIOGRAPHY

"Actively Try the Method of Investing in Capital Construction with Loans" (editorial). People's Daily, December 12, 1979. Reproduced in Foreign Broadcast Information Service, Daily Report, no. 242 (December 14, 1979), p. L10.

Allen, George, and Audrey Donnithorne. Western Enterprise in Far Eastern Economic Development: China and Japan. London: Macmillan, 1954.

"Asian Bonanza." Wall Street Journal, October 19, 1978, p. 1.

Awanohara, Susumu. "China's Deficit Here to Stay." Far Eastern Economic Review, June 20, 1975, pp. 36-37.

_____. "When Japan Deposits, China Borrows." Far Eastern Economic Review, June 17, 1974, pp. 42-45.

Bailey, Martin. "Chinese Aid in Action." In Chinese Road to Development, edited by Neville Maxwell, 2d ed., pp. 289-97. London: Pergamon, 1979.

Bank of China. "The Bank of China's Work of International Settlements." Foreign Trade of the PRC 1 (1962): 4.

"Bank of China Looks Ahead." Financial Times, July 4, 1978, p. 4.

"Bank of China Signs Agreement with UK for $300 Million Deposit." Globe and Mail, December 8, 1978, p. B2.

"Bank of China: Still a Touch of Glamour." Financial Times, June 10, 1977, p. 29.

Batsavage, Richard, and John Davie. "China's International Trade and Finance." In Chinese Economy Post-Mao, U.S., Congress, Joint Economic Committee, pp. 707-41. Washington, D.C.: Government Printing Office, 1978.

Baxter, A. J. "Origins of British Exchange Banks in China." Economic History, a supplement of Economic Journal, January 1934.

Bennett, Gordon. "The Emerging Business Climate." East Asian Executive Reports 2 (March 1980): 3, 15-16.

_____. China's Finance and Trade. New York: Sharpe, 1978.

Bonavia, David. "Another Turnaround in China." Far Eastern Economic Review, December 12, 1980, p. 60.

_____. "Signs of Inflation Are Manifest Today." Far Eastern Economic Review, September 26, 1980, p. 48.

Carlson, Steven. "Expropriated Property, Frozen Assets, and Sovereign Immunity: Legal Aspects to United States-China Trade Relations." Columbia Journal of Transnational Law 15 (1976): 254.

"Cashing in on China's Oil Boom." Far Eastern Review, November 14, 1980, pp. 52-54.

Cassou, Pierre-Henri. "The Chinese Monetary System." Chinese Economic Studies 9 (1975/76): 82-97. Reprinted in China Quarterly, July 1974, pp. 559-66.

Chang, Yen-nian. "Financing Possibilities." In China's New Economic Strategies, pp. 123-330. Switzerland: Zentrung für Unterneh-mungsfuhrung [Economic Management Center], 1980.

Chao, Kuo-Chun, ed. Economic Planning and Organization in Mainland China, vol. 1. Cambridge, Mass.: Harvard Center for East-Asian Studies, 1959.

Cheng, Chu-yüan. Monetary Affairs of Communist China. Communist China Problem Research Series. Hong Kong: Union Research Institute, 1954.

Chi, Ts'ai-ch'eng. Concise Treatise on Comprehensive Financial Planning. Beijing: People's Republic of China, 1961.

"China: An Export Strategy to Pay for Modernization." Business Week, January 15, 1979, p. 48.

"China and Hong Kong in Joint Property Deal." Financial Times, August 31, 1978, p. 1.

"China and Japan: Aid Precedes Trade." Economist, December 8, 1979, pp. 71-72.

"China: Showing a New Face to Business." Times (London), October 24, 1978, p. 18.

"China: Signs of Possible Emergence." Financial Times, May 30, 1978, p. 34.

"China Trade and Investment: Exports Please." Economist, July 14, 1979, p. 78.

"Chinese Bonds: Fujian Puts Out a Feeler." Economist, February 2, 1980, p. 86.

"Chinese Borrowing on the International Capital Markets." International Currency Review 11 (1979): 47-49.

Ching, Tsai. "Our Country Is Now a Socialist Country without Internal or External Debts." Peking Review, May 23, 1969, pp. 15-17.

Collis, Maurice. Wayfong: The Hong Kong and Shanghai Banking Corporation. London: Hong Kong Bank, 1965.

Cooper, John F. China's Foreign Aid: An Instrument of Peking's Foreign Policy. Lexington, Mass.: Lexington Books, 1976.

Dahlby, Tracy. "A Cautious Helping Hand." Far Eastern Economic Review, December 14, 1979, p. 100.

_____. "Japan's China Extravaganza." Far Eastern Economic Review, November 16, 1979, pp. 56-58.

"Deals on Ice." China Trade Report 17 (April 1979): 12-13.

Denny, David L. "China's Foreign Financial Liabilities." U.S.-China Business Review 2 (January-February 1975): 34-38.

_____. "International Finance in the People's Republic of China." In China: A Reassessment of the Economy, U.S., Congress, Joint Economic Committee, pp. 653-877. Washington, D.C.: Government Printing Office, 1975.

Denny, David L., and Frederic M. Surls. "China's Foreign Financial Liabilities." China Business Review 4 (March-April 1977): 10-12.

_____. "Recent Developments in the International Financial Policies of the People's Republic of China." Stanford Journal of International Studies 10 (1975): 163-86.

Donnithorne, Audrey. "Aspects of Neo-Liuist Economic Policy." Australian Journal of Chinese Affairs 3 (1980): 27-39.

_____. China's Economic System. New York: Praeger, 1967.

_____. "China's Economic System." Three Banks Review 103 (September 1974): 3-25.

_____. "China's Import of Capital Goods and Policy on Foreign Credit: 1972-1974." Australian Economic Papers 16 (June 1977): 1-25.

Dreamer, Deidra. "Bank of China in a New Financial Role." East Asian Executive Reports 1 (September 1979): 17-19.

_____. "Recent Financial Developments in China." East Asian Executive Reports 1 (October 15, 1979): 12-16.

_____. "Understanding the Bank of China's Letter of Credit Practices." East Asian Exeuctive Reports 1 (November 1979): 3, 19-20.

Ecklund, George. "Banking and Finance." In China: A Handbook, edited by Yuan-li Wa, pp. 579-94. New York: Praeger, 1973.

Eckstein, Alexander. China's Economic Revolution. Cambridge: At the University Press, 1977.

"Economic Development in the Chinese People's Republic." International Currency Review 11 (1979): 50-60.

Endacott, G. B. A History of Hong Kong. 2d ed. Hong Kong: Oxford University Press, 1973.

Fairbank, John K., Edwin O. Reischauer, and Albert Craig. East Asia: The Modern Transformation. Boston: Houghton Mifflin, 1965.

Fairhill, Lawrence. "A Peek into Peking's Banks." Finance 89 (October 1971): 28-31, 65, 69.

Feintech, Lynn. "The Role of International Trade and Finance in the People's Republic of China." In A New Look at Legal Aspects of Doing Business with China, edited by Howard M. Holtzmann and Walter S. Surrey, pp. 381-405. New York: Practising Law Institute, 1979.

"Financing the New Customer." Banker 49 (December 1978): 45-53.

"First Chicago Reaches to Win Peking's Favor." Business Week, October 17, 1977, p. 36.

Fry, Richard. "China's Financing Prospects." Banker 124 (December 1974): 1487-90.

Goldring, Mary. "Tea at the Bank of China." Euromoney 11 (March 1979): 65-67.

Goodstadt, Leo. "Peking Elevates the Bank of China's Status." Euromoney 11 (September 1979): 66-67.

_____. "Peking's Firm Hold on the Money Supply." Far Eastern Economic Review, June 13, 1975, pp. 39-40.

_____. "Why Bankers Have Become Heroes in China." Euromoney 11 (January 1979): 79-85.

Goodstadt, Leo, and Pamela Clarke. "Foreign Banks and Chinese Loans: The Awakening Giant of the East." Euromoney 10 (October 1978): 68-79.

Hare, Paul G. "China's System of Economic Planning." Mimeographed. University of Stirling, 1980.

Harrison, Selig. China, Oil and Asia Conflict Ahead? New York: Columbia University Press, 1977.

Hawten, G. "Traders Look to Steady Rise." Times (London), March 21, 1973, p. iii.

Henderson, Dan, and Tasuku Matsuo. "Trade with Japan." In Law and Politics in China's Foreign Trade, edited by Victor Li, pp. 28-69. Seattle: University of Washington Press, 1971.

Howe, Christopher. China's Economy—A Basic Guide. London: Elek Books, 1978.

Hsiao, Gene T. The Foreign Trade of China: Policy, Law, and Practice. Berkeley: University of California Press, 1977.

Hsiao, Katherine Huang. Money and Monetary Policy in Communist China. New York: Columbia University Press, 1971.

Hughes, Richard. Borrowed Place, Borrowed Time. 2d ed. Hong Kong: André Deutsch, 1976.

Hung, Fred C. "The Role of Money and Credit in Communist China's Economic Planning." In East Asian Occasional Papers, vol. 1, edited by Harry Lamley, pp. 51-67. Honolulu: University of Hawaii, 1969.

Hung, Ta. "The Principles Governing Bank Loans and Their Relation to Currency Circulation." Ching Chi Yenchiu [Economic research] (Peking), 1962.

"Is China a Non-Event for Bankers? Yes . . . and No." Far Eastern Economic Review, September 19, 1980, pp. 73-74.

Jao, Y. C. Banking and Currency in Hong Kong. London: Macmillan, 1974.

Japan External Trade Organization. How to Approach the China Market. New York: John Wiley & Sons, 1972.

Jayakumar, S. "The Singapore Branch of the Bank of China and Exercise of 'Extra-territorial Rights.'" American Journal of International Law 64 (1970): 371-74.

Jones, P. H. M. "People's Banking." Far Eastern Economic Review, July 15, 1965, p. 137.

Kaplan, Frederic M., Julian Sobin, and Stephen Anders. Encyclopedia of China Today. New York: Eurasia Press, 1979.

King, Frank H. Money and Monetary Policy in China, 1845-1895. Washington, D.C.: Howard University Press, 1965.

Klatt, Werner. "China's New Economic Policy: A Statistical Appraisal." China Quarterly, December 1980, pp. 716-33.

Klingenburg, Martin, and Joseph Pattison. "Joint Ventures in the People's Republic of China: The New Legal Environment." Virginia Journal of International Law 19 (1979): 807-39.

Kraar, Louis. "Beijing's Overseas Chinese Connection." Asia 2 (July-August 1979): 4-7, 36-37.

_____. "China: Trying the Market Way." Fortune, December 31, 1979, pp. 51-54.

Kramer, Barry. "Borrowing from Capitalism." Wall Street Journal, May 8, 1979, p. 40.

_____. "People's Banker." Wall Street Journal, December 1, 1976, p. 1.

Lauriat, George. "Hope beneath the Sea." Far Eastern Economic Review, March 6, 1980, pp. 41-42.

Lee, Dinah. "China Joins the Money Club." South (prepublication issue), August 1980, pp. 52-53.

_____. "Trade Follows the Loans." Far Eastern Economic Review, May 29, 1981, pp. 49-50.

Lewis, Christopher. "China's Banks: The Communist Capitalists." Far Eastern Economic Review, April 1, 1974, pp. 17-18.

Li, Hsien-nien. "Some Problems in the Practical Aspects of Financial Administration and Credit Provision." Hung Chi [Red flag] 1 (1960): 10-12.

Li, Hui-min. "Money and Banking on the Chinese Mainland." Chinese Communist Affairs 4 (February 1967): 34-44.

Li, Victor, ed. Law and Politics in China's Foreign Trade. Seattle: University of Washington Press, 1971.

Lieberthal, Kenneth. "China: The Politics behind the New Economics." Fortune 100 (December 31, 1979): 44-50.

Lin, Chi-K'en. "On the Operation of the Laws Governing Currency Circulation under a Socialist System." Ching Chi Yenchiu [Economic research] (Peking), no. 2 (1963).

Liu, Melinda. "China Will Stay Cautious despite a U.S.$60 Billion Credit." Far Eastern Economic Review, October 5, 1979, pp. 75-77.

_____. "Financing the New Customer." Banker 128 (December 1978): 49-52.

_____. "For China's Partners a Confident Future." Far Eastern Economic Review, September 7, 1979, pp. 40-41.

_____. "Hong Kong Banking: China Makes Its Presence Felt." Financial Times, July 19, 1978, p. 28.

_____. "Rock-Bottom Terms Are a Must for Foreigners." Far Eastern Economic Review, September 21, 1979, pp. 61-63.

Loong, Pauline. "Capitalizing on New-Socialism." Far Eastern Economic Review, August 15, 1980, pp. 40-42.

Lubman, Stanley. "Contracts, Practice and Law in Trade with China: Some Observations." In Chinese Economy Post-Mao, U.S., Congress, Joint Economic Committee, vol. 1. Washington, D.C.: Government Printing Office, 1978.

_____. "The Emergence of New Institutions for Trade and Investment in China." In Private Investors Abroad: 1979, edited by the Southwestern Legal Foundation, pp. 189-244. New York: Matthew Bender, 1979.

_____. "Sino-American Trade: Legal and Practical Problems and Prospects." In Current Legal Aspects of Doing Business with Sino-Soviet Nations, edited by James T. Haight, pp. 66-80. Chicago: American Bar Association, 1973.

_____. "Trade between the United States and the People's Republic of China." Law and Policy in International Business 8 (1976): 1-38.

Ludlow, Nicholas. "China's Oil." U.S.-China Business Review 1 (January-February 1974).

Ludlow, Nicholas, and James Stepanek. "Inside the Bank of China." China Business Review 7 (July-August 1980): 9-13.

Lupton, Edward. "Hong Kong's Role in Sino-Western Trade." In China's Trade with the West, edited by Arthur A. Stahnke, p. 201. New York: Praeger, 1972.

MacDougall, Colina. "China Learns from East Europe's Economic Reforms." Financial Times, November 14, 1980, p. 31.

MacDougall, Colina, and David Marsh. "Peking Learns the Art of Playing the Bullion Market." Financial Times, December 18, 1980, p. 4.

Meyerhoff, Arthur A. "Petroleum Industry—Geology Reserves Technology and Policies." In China Trade: Prospects and Perspectives, edited by David C. Buxbaum, Cassondra E. Joseph, and Paul D. Reynolds. New York: Praeger, 1982.

Miyashita, Tadao. The Currency and Financial System of Mainland China. Translated by T. R. McEwan. Seattle: University of Washington Press, 1966.

Mulkern, Louis. "The Financial Aspects of China Trade." In Trade with China, edited by the American Management Association, pp. 17-25. New York: American Management Association, 1972.

Neilan, Edward, and Charles R. Smith. The Future of the China Market. Washington, D. C.: American Enterprise Institute for Public Policy Research, 1974.

Perkins, Dwight. Market Control and Planning in Communist China. Cambridge, Mass.: Harvard University Press, 1966.

_____. "Price Stability and Development in Mainland China (1951-63)." Journal of Political Economy 72 (1964): 364-75.

Prybyla, Jan S. The Chinese Economy, Problems and Policies. Columbia: University of South Carolina Press, 1978.

Rafferty, Kevin. "Hong Kong and China." Financial Times, June 15, 1981, p. v.

Reese, K. "Mainland China and Western Trade Credits." Intereconomics 2 (1976): 45-53.

Reghizzi, Gabriele C. "Legal Aspects of Trade with China: The Italian Experience." Harvard International Law Journal 9 (1968): 108.

Reynolds, Paul D. "Doing Business with the People's Republic of China: Tax Considerations." International Lawyer 14 (1980): 49-72.

_____. "The Joint Venture Law of the People's Republic of China: Preliminary Observations." International Lawyer 14 (1980): 31-47.

_____. "Legal Framework of Sino-U.S. Trade." In Trade with the People's Republic of China: The January Briefing, pp. 80-109. Houston: Rice University, 1979.

_____. "The Role of Law in China's Modernization." Poly Law Review 6 (1980): 12-20.

Schwering, Katherine. "Financing Imports from China." United States-China Business Review 1 (1974): 36-40.

Shields, Roger, Paul Spooner, and Sandi Summerlin. "Financing Sales to China." In A New Look at Legal Aspects of Doing Business with China, edited by Howard M. Holtzmann and

Walter Sterling Surrey, pp. 407-36. New York: Practising Law Institute, 1979.

Smith, A. H. "Mainland Chinese Banks." Eurocurrency, vol. 4 (1972).

Smith, Charles. "China May Not Use Japan Credits for Plant Imports." Financial Times, March 2, 1981, p. 3.

_____. "The Future for China's Trade." Banker 122 (February 1972): 157-65.

Starr, Robert I., and Julius Kaplan. "The Legal Framework of China Trade." In Doing Business with China: American Trade Opportunities in the 1970's, edited by William W. Whitson, pp. 379-97. New York: Praeger, 1974.

"Steel Industry Plans to Give China 150-Day Usuance for December Shipments." Japan Economic Journal, January 14, 1975, p. 4.

Stepanek, James. "Beijing's Continuing Retrenchment." China Business Review 8 (January-February 1981): 16-18.

_____. "China Joins the Money Club." South (prepublication issue) August 1980, pp. 52-53.

_____. "Fujian Bonds?" China Business Review 7 (March-April 1980): 54.

_____. "How Are China's Exchange Rates Set?" U.S.-China Business Review 3 (January-February 1976): 11.

_____. "A Ten-Year Profile of the Bank of China." China Business Review 6 (September-October 1979): 35-44.

Theroux, Eugene A. "China's Foreign Trade: Principles, Institutions and Performance." In Post-Mao China and U.S. China Trade, edited by Shao-chuan Land, pp. 55-58. Charlottesville: University Press of Virginia, 1977.

"Troubled Talks." Asian Wall Street Journal Weekly, February 18, 1980, p. 13.

Tsiang, S. C. "Money and Banking in Communist China." In An Economic Profile of Mainland China, U.S., Congress, Joint Economic Committee, vol. 1, pp. 323-39. Washington, D.C.: Government Printing Office, 1967.

"UK Banks Negotiate Finance Possibly Totaling $750 Million." Times (London), August 25, 1978, p. 13.

"The Uncontrollable Stateless Money." Far Eastern Economic Review, September 21, 1979, pp. 44-50.

U.S., Congress, Joint Economic Committee. China: A Reassessment of the Economy. Washington, D.C.: Government Printing Office, 1975.

U.S., Congress, House, Committee on International Relations. A New Realism: Factfinding Mission to the People's Republic of China, July 3-13, 1978. Washington, D.C.: Government Printing Office, 1978.

U.S., Consulate General. China's Financial Dilemma—Budget Trends, 1978-1981. Hong Kong: Consulate General, November 1980.

U.S., Department of Commerce. Doing Business with China. Washington, D.C.: Government Printing Office, 1979.

"U.S. Trade with China: Prospects through 1985." Business America 2 (February 1979): 3-7.

Whitson, William W., ed. Doing Business with China: American Trade Opportunities in the 1970's. New York: Praeger, 1974.

Wilson, Dick. "Bank of China in Singapore." Banker, vol. 122, (February 1972).

_____. "The Bank of China Steps Out." Banker 124 (February 1974): 105-10.

_____. "The Bank of China's Expanding Role in International Finances." United States-China Business Review 1 (June 1974): 21-26.

_____. "How Banks Work in China." Banker 130 (January 1980): 19-27.

_____. "Overseas Chinese Banking Corporation." Banker 126 (December 1976): 1468-70.

Wolfers, Nicholas. "Financing the China Trade." In Trading with China, edited by Colina MacDougall, pp. 95-117. London: McGraw-Hill, 1980.

Wrightman, Alistair. "How Japan Finances Trade with China." U.S.-China Business Review 2 (March-April 1975): 30-93.

Wyles, John. "China Turns to U.N. in Food Crisis." Financial Times, March 9, 1981, p. 22.

Yang, Pei-hsin. "China's Stable Monetary System." Peking Review, June 25, 1965, pp. 15-19.

Yang, Po. "New China's Policy." Peking Review, November 20, 1964.

INDEX

ABOUT THE AUTHOR

PAUL D. REYNOLDS is an Associate Professor of Law at the Texas Tech University School of Law. His primary professional interests are in the legal and financial problems of developing nations and their relationship to the international banking system. His previous books are International Community Agreements and the Common Fund: A Legal and Financial Analysis and China Trade: Prospects and Perspectives, both published by Praeger. He studied law at Trinity College, University of Dublin, and Columbia University. He is currently associated with the law firm of Fulbright and Jaworski in Houston and London.